Seven Statements of Survival

Conversations with Dance Professionals

Edited and with introductions by
Renata Celichowska

Dance & Movement Press™

New York

Published in 2008 by Rosen Book Works, LLC
29 East 21st Street, New York, NY 10010

Copyright © 2008 by Renata Celichowska

First Edition

Editor: Renata Celichowska
Book Design: Greg Tucker

Library of Congress Cataloging-in-Publication Data

Seven statements of survival : conversations with dance professionals / edited and with introductions by Renata Celichowska.
    p. cm.
  Includes index.
  ISBN-13: 978-1-4042-9716-6 (hardcover)
  ISBN-13: 978-1-4042-9720-3 (pbk.)
  1. Dancers--Interviews. 2. Choreographers--Interviews. 3. Dance teachers--Interviews. 4. Dance. I. Celichowska, Renata.
  GV1785.A1 S47 2008
  792.80280922--dc22
  [B]

                        2007024119

Manufactured in Malaysia

Table of Contents

ILLUSTRATIONS

ACKNOWLEDGMENTS

The honesty and generosity of the seven people in this collection of interviews was a special gift. Thank you Deborah, Carolyn, Andrea, Garth, Joann, Bill, and Madeleine. I am left with a collection of special pearls from each of you. Thank you Garth for your passion and warmth; Deborah for your piercing clarity that comes with a glimmer in your eye; Andrea for your energy and pragmatic outlook; Carolyn for your uncompromising individuality and joie de vivre; Bill for your openness and valuable insight; Joann for your profound simplicity; and Madeleine for your selfless objectivity. I am honored to have been entrusted with your stories and will continue to enjoy the memory of my time with all of you.

As the hidden force behind this project, Nancy Allison has provided unending enthusiasm, support, patience, and friendship throughout the book's conception, execution, and completion. The following interviews could literally not have been done without her. Thank you Nancy for gently, yet persistently, urging me forward.

I send an eternal thank-you to all of my many teachers, both of writing and dance, from all parts of my life. Thank you Deborah Willard, Leo Grant, Genevieve Oswald, and Ernestine Stodelle for valuing and imparting your love of good writing to me.

My circle of friends, professional colleagues, and family give me endless encouragement on all my adventures. Since beginning this project four years ago, my own life has undergone profound changes, and through it all, this tribe of people has always been there to support me. Thank you Julia, Tim, Deb, Chris, Patti, Tom, Mimi, Bob, Edward, and Kathryn. Continued love to my parents, Krystyna and Stefan; my sisters, Ewa and Misia; and to John, Charlie, Alexandra, Stefan, Isabel, Peter, and Doris. My family is my foundation. And finally, a thank-you to my new family, Charles, my husband, and Casimir, our beautiful son. Life certainly is full of wonderful surprises, and you two are the best surprise of all!

Renata Celichowska

FOREWARD

Many years ago, as an undergraduate dance major at Ohio University in the sleepy Appalachian hill town of Athens, Ohio, I was wandering through the college bookstore when I happened upon a paperback copy of Selma Jeanne Cohen's landmark book *The Modern Dance: Seven Statements of Belief.* On the black-and-white cover, a shadowy Paul Taylor was swinging an even more shadowy female dancer around his hip. Inside, Taylor, José Limón, Anna Sokolow, Erick Hawkins, Donald McKayle, Alwin Nikolais, and Pauline Koner shared their passionate, intellectual, humorous, or spiritual vision of what they believed modern dance to be. Seven distinct and stimulating voices to think about, quote from, emulate, or reject. *Seven Statements*, as it was often called among the cognoscenti, was a secret bible of the aspiring and faithful for my generation of modern dancers. We kept it on our bookshelves and close to our hearts.

Thirty years later, after a career in dance as a performer, choreographer, teacher, and now an editor, I found myself again thinking about Cohen's brilliant book. In the spring of 2003, I proposed to Renata Celichowska that we create an homage to the little book that had inspired so many bright-eyed, inquisitive young dancers. As colleagues teaching in the Dance Education Program at New York University, we were keenly aware that while today's dancers, from undergraduate to doctoral candidates, were as passionate as we had been, they had different concerns. They wondered how they were going to thrive or even survive in this difficult field. Should they stay in New York or launch their career somewhere else? What would they do when they stopped performing? How would they cope if they didn't turn out to be the choreographer or dancer they had dreamed of being? How could they have a life in dance if they didn't necessarily want to be a performer or a choreographer?

With this in mind, we created a list of ideal subjects, exemplary professionals with stories to tell and wisdom to share. And to our surprise, they all accepted our invitation to participate in the Sevens Project, as we had begun to call it. Then we designed a list of questions that we hoped would stimulate their memories of the past, provoke their assessment and concerns of the present, and bring forth their hopes for the future. Renata herself was exemplary in her courage and fearlessness as she crossed the globe, on less than a shoestring budget, with cassette player in hand, meeting, talking, and recording. The result of her work is this new volume that captures in a totally fresh and original way seven distinct and stimulating voices from a dance world, bigger and more varied than Cohen could have imagined in 1965. I like to think she would be happy to know that her groundbreaking work spawned this child. I hope it will inspire new generations of dancers to follow their passion and bring their own unique voices and visions to the ever-growing, ever-changing, ever-frustrating, ever-beautiful world of dance.

Nancy Allison
Editorial Director
Dance & Movement Press

INTRODUCTION

What are dance professionals and where do they come from?

Where do I go from here and how can I "survive" in the dance world are questions that almost every dancer asks at some point in his or her career. These challenges have come up time and time again throughout my "dance life," amounting to something like a love-hate melodrama at times. Like many people in the dance field, I spent a good portion of my early years running between home, school, and the dance studio. I learned how to take a class and put my hair up in a variety of classical ballet styles. But my perspective on the dance world was surprisingly narrow. I had this rigid notion that being "successful" meant I would train for X amount of years, then perform with one of maybe five major dance companies; otherwise, I would quit.

It was only after my own struggles, first as a dancer, then as a scholar, teacher, and choreographer, that I discovered that I had more options available than I could have ever imagined. With each new experience—whether it be during my graduate studies, as a dancer with the Erick Hawkins Dance Company, training with special dance mentors, or poring over dance archives at the New York Public Library—the dance world gradually became bigger and bigger. This expansion renewed my respect for it and for myself. I was no longer daunted by the cocktail party question, "Oh, you're a dancer. So, what do you really do for a living?" Instead, I began to welcome the opportunity to address the question. Unwittingly, I became an advocate for the dance field. I also realized that I needed to be an advocate, and a knowledgeable one at that, in order to prosper in the dance world.

Nevertheless, surviving in the dance world seems just short of impossible. The hours are long. The monetary compensation is dismal. The job market, if it exists at all, is unstable. In our culture, there still is a vague prejudice against dance as a legitimate profession that creates a frustrating haze around the brilliant work and efforts of dancers and dance professionals, often undermining our own opinions of ourselves.

It doesn't take much effort, however, to find dance-related or dance-influenced professions that are equally important parts of the dance field. For example, knowledgeable dance administrators direct college, community, and professional service organizations throughout the country. Dance historians, notators, videographers, and anthropologists work to preserve culturally significant dances on the verge of extinction. Lawyers and labor professionals help dancers and choreographers in their struggle with copyright laws, with health insurance issues, and generally to achieve equal status with comparable artists in other fields. Dancers with refined knowledge of their bodies share it with average Americans suffering from physical ailments, often due simply to ignorance or misconceptions about their own physicality. These and other dance-related professions offer countless options to dancers. In fact, they constitute a vital part of the U.S. arts economy.

Even though these professions benefit from employing knowledgeable dancers, the dancers are often the last to hear about them. Therefore, the more those dancers know about dance-related professions and the struggles and successes of those working in them, the more they can find affirmation or guidance for their own futures. In this way our entire dance community flourishes.

This need to acknowledge and affirm all our dance greats was the impetus behind the following conversations with seven dance professionals. Since the 1980s, researchers in dance have filled in crucial gaps in the world's dance literature. Dancers, dance professionals, and people interested in dance can now read about the lives of not only the most obvious dance heroes, like Nijinsky, Duncan, Balanchine, or Graham, but also other significant dance greats. Dance greats who are performers or choreographers but also presenters, fund-raisers, writers, physical therapists, master teachers, and researchers. The list goes on. The following interviews are another contribution to this growing library of our collective dance consciousness.

The seven individuals interviewed in this book represent a cross section of the dance world. They are people who have found a way to live a rewarding life in dance. Garth Fagan emigrated from Jamaica and found his artistic home in the United States. Carolyn Carlson left the United States and evolved her artistic life in Europe. Deborah Jowitt made her way to writing about dance from her work as a dancer and choreographer. In contrast, Andrea Snyder struggled to combine her love of dance with the need to make a living, discovering along the way that she could be an advocate for dance on a national level and support herself. Bill Evans relates his extraordinary story of self-awakening as a dancer, choreographer, and master teacher. Joann Keali'inohomoku tells an equally remarkable story of how her childhood dream to provide a bridge between cultures through dance has lasted as a passion to this day. Finally, Madeleine Nichols, a longtime dance curator, reveals a depth and breadth of understanding about dance that points toward its brilliant future.

The seven interviews took place between February and September 2004. Since the initial interviews, the seven artists presented in this book have gone on to other projects and personal life events. However, the ideas that they shared during these generous conversations are no less pertinent, powerful, and thought provoking than when we first spoke.

The interviews were inspiring for me. Each spurred me on to the next. As I spoke to each artist, I often recognized parallel experiences in my life or discovered that we shared similar opinions about a subject dear to my heart. I often heard the same names mentioned in more than one interview, making me reflect upon what was personal, generational, or universal in our discussions. These overlapping ideas strengthened my belief that the dance community is a true community and that dancers, regardless of generation, origin, or geographic location, share a common dance heritage and language.

Did the conversations give me any concrete solutions about how to proceed in my own dance life? No. But they did do what I had hoped they would do. They opened my horizons and my perspective on dance again, making me admire even more what dance professionals and dance lovers do. It is a vast world, inhabited by an impressive array of movers, thinkers, dreamers, workers, and visionaries.

As part of many dance practices, the dancer finds center by invoking the many directions in a personal sphere surrounding him- or herself. The East, South, West, and North, the Heavens, and Earth are all honored. They emanate from and return back to the core. So, at this midlife juncture, I look to an older generation for guidance based on hard-won knowledge, to current practitioners for other perspectives, to a younger generation for inspiration, and back to my own unique experience as a way of understanding where I am now. In one of Erick Hawkins's last dances, *Killer-of-Enemies*, he paraphrased, as part of a spoken dialogue, a Navajo invocation. It reads: "Oh, beauty before me, beauty behind me, beauty to the right of me, beauty to the left of me, beauty above me, beauty below me, I am on the pollen path." It is toward this idea of beauty for all of our dance lives that I move.

The seven individuals interviewed for this book are all exceptional leaders in their areas of expertise. May they inspire you as they have me. Each of them has a unique story to share. Yet, the essential message is the same from all of them. The dance world is comprised of a myriad of professions and options. Follow your passion for it, and it will provide a space for you. Dance needs you as much as you need it.

— R.C.

© Helge Reistad

Deborah Jowitt

DEBORAH JOWITT

"I cry when I read really beautiful dance writing."

Known as one of America's foremost dance writers and critics, Deborah Jowitt came to writing through her extensive experience as a performer and choreographer. Jowitt began her professional dance career in 1953, performing with a wide variety of dance and theater artists. In 1963, she danced and choreographed as an original member of Dance Theater Workshop and continued to perform and choreograph as she developed her reputation as a writer. In addition to her early contributions to the WBAI 1960s radio series *The Critical People*, Jowitt has been a dance critic for the *Village Voice* since 1967 and has published numerous important dance works, including *Dance Beat* (1977); *The Dance in Mind* (1985); *Time and the Dancing Image* (1988), which was awarded the de la Torre Bueno Prize; and most recently, *Jerome Robbins: His Life, His Theater, His Dance* (2004). Jowitt has been teaching for New York University's Tisch School of the Arts since 1975 and has guest lectured at the University of Copenhagen, Harvard University, Princeton University, the London Contemporary School of Dance, and the Theatre Academy in Helsinki. Jowitt's awards include a Bessie Award (1985), the American Dance Guild's annual award (1991), and the Dance Critics Association Award (2006).

SETTING THE SCENE

I joined Deborah in the intimacy of her West Village home on a cool March afternoon. I had been an admirer of Deborah's writing since studying dance criticism in 1986 with Ernestine Stodelle at New York University. Since that time, Deborah's writing has always been for me an ideal toward which to strive, and I was eager and honored to finally be meeting and speaking with her in person. The afternoon flowed like Deborah's words, steadily and elegantly, as the family cat roamed in and out of our conversation. A preview copy of her soon-to-be published book on Jerome Robbins lay on the table near the couch. I had entered a world of simple candor, intellectual curiosity, but most important of all, the world of a fulfilled and dedicated artist.

— R.C.

Q: How do you describe what you do to people who aren't in the dance world, maybe children or laypeople?

DJ: Well, what I do is [*chuckle*] I write about dance. I attend a performance, I absorb it, I think about it, and then I try to write about it in words that somehow reflect it. So that I give some sense of what a dance was like and what I felt while I was watching it.

Q: And do you consider your involvement with dance to be your profession, your career, your work, a passion, a calling, all of the above? None of the above?

DJ: Well, it's all those things. It is my profession. It's the way I make a living of some sort. I don't know if I would say it was a calling because it happened that I just fell into writing, having been a dancer and a choreographer. I didn't wake up one morning and say, "It's my mission to write." Writing criticism simply evolved out of what I was doing through a series of very fortuitous coincidences. And when I began to write, I didn't consider myself a *writer*. I was who I was, and I was writing about dance. It wasn't a sudden thing, but suddenly I became aware that I was this writer, I was this critic. People sent me invitations to come to their performances.

So it's not like a calling to the church. But as I wrote more and more, criticism became more and more part of my life and full of obligations: to see this, to cover that, to be fair to this, to remember that I hadn't seen so-and-so's work for a number of years. Once writing criticism becomes a profession and not just something that you enjoy doing, but something for which you are paid, the responsibilities of the job come down on you. But I've been writing about dance for the *Voice* since 1967, so I must *like* it, right? I find it exciting to do.

Q: How did you first get introduced to dance? And what are some of the landmark events in your dance/dance writing life? I use *dance* in the larger sense.

DJ: Gosh, I don't know. I studied dancing like a lot of little girls do. I think originally my parents sent me for ballet lessons because my feet were flat. It was supposed to be good for me, along with picking up marbles with my toes and walking on beach sand. It was fun, and I liked it. I kept taking classes with better and better teachers, but I didn't practice and I wasn't serious about it.

Then, when I was a teenager, I wanted very much to be an actress. So, one summer I took a course at a local little theater. And one of the components of the course was called Body Work, which turned out to be modern dance. And I liked it.

Q: Where was this?

DJ: It was in Los Angeles. I liked it very much. And the woman who taught it, Harriette Ann Gray—who had been a member of the Humphrey-Weidman Company—and her husband, an acting teacher, told me they thought I had a lot of talent for dancing and I should come to the Perry-Mansfield summer camp in Steamboat Springs, Colorado, where they both taught. I didn't realize at the time that they got twenty-five dollars for every student they managed to refer! So I got a partial scholarship there and continued to study with Harriette Ann, and eventually I was asked to join her company. And then, I was a dancer. That was it!

Her company transferred to New York at that point, and it dissolved after I had danced with it for two years. So here I was in New York, all by myself with no commitments. The Harriette Ann Gray Company had had a very big schedule of classes and rehearsals and tour dates and all that. So I had to find a job and places to dance because, you know, I was a *dancer*.

So it wasn't like I woke up at the age of eight and said, "I am going to be a ballerina."

Q: It just happened.

DJ: It happened that suddenly...also, I had spent a year in England trying to get work as an actress. I was young, but I was large and dark and the ingénue parts that I could play were not parts that I looked right for. That had been rather frustrating. So to come back and be asked to join Harriette Ann's company sort of validated my being good at something. I didn't have to run around to agents and try to find auditions. I was appreciated for something I could do well. I didn't have to prove myself. So, you couldn't exactly say that I became a dancer by default, but there certainly was a change from acting to dancing.

Q: Were there other influential people along your path, either as dancers, choreographers, or writers, with whom you worked whom you remember as major inspirations?

DJ: Well, I worked with many choreographers of that generation after Graham, you know, Sophie Maslow, Pearl Lang, Mary Anthony, and Pauline Koner. And learned from all of them. Pauline taught me a great deal about how to perform. She was very sensitive to the nuances of performing in a way that other people that I had worked with were not. I remember we used to stand endlessly trying to feel the air on the back of our hands in a certain gesture. She would say, "Like this. Like this." [*gesture of hand pressing gently through air*] She was not easy to get on with, but she was not negative. She was just very picky! I learned a lot from her.

And then, in the 1960s, I worked for a while at Valerie Bettis's studio, and she was extremely wise about critiquing other people's choreography. She said things to me about my choreography that were revelations in some way. Very simple things like, "How come your phrases don't ever cross over the bar line?" and "When the music's in 4/4, each of your units lasts only four counts." Things like that were very important for me to hear at the time.

Also, I was one of the early members of Dance Theater Workshop [DTW] when it was much more of a collective. We put on evenings and danced in each other's choreography. The people I worked with there—Rudy Perez, Jamie Cunningham, Tina Croll, Art Bauman, Jack Moore, Jeff Duncan, and others—were part of that sixties ferment, even though few of us were as far out as the Judson[1] people. That atmosphere was very stimulating to be around.

In terms of writing, I would say…it was Marcia Siegel who got me started writing. She had heard me on a radio program that a friend of mine had put together for the Pacifica Foundation-WBAI here. It was called *The Critical People*. So my first work in criticism was writing and delivering five-minute reviews on the radio along with these other critical people. There'd be somebody talking about music and somebody talking about books. There was also a movie person, a drama person, and so on, and then we would have discussions about one another's topics. We'd all try to see or read what the others were reviewing. It was very exciting.

So, Marcia heard me on the radio. She was editing *Dance Scope* at that time, and she asked me if I would write. I think the first thing I wrote for her was a review of Edwin Denby's *Dancers, Buildings and People in the Streets*. And of course that was a revelation. Through a series of coincidences, I shortly started writing for the *Voice*.

I became more involved in the writing as I began to be taken seriously as a critic. And I thought about what I considered good writing and whose writing I liked to read. I started reading a lot. At the same time, I was educating myself in dance history, because I had no background in that. Like many people then, I didn't have a college degree in dance.

Q: This was while you were also choreographing? I ask this because it seems that from your generation of dancers, practicing making dance was part and parcel of also being a performer.

DJ: Well, in modern dance at that time, there was a sort of cycle. The dancer-choreographer ran the company. And if you were in that person's company, you never got the lead because *she* always had the lead. Or if you were a man, you were her mate and you rarely got to express yourself. I mean you danced, and maybe you had wonderful opportunities to dance, but it was sort of assumed that the way to advance was to become one of those dancer-choreographers and star yourself in your own work, which people did. I started out misguidedly doing that and made some really bad choreography.

But I think that concept changed gradually. A lot of people began to see that they didn't necessarily need to feature themselves in their choreography and that they could perhaps make better work if they didn't. I mean, there are still people, Trisha Brown for example, wonderful dancers, who perform in their own works. But I think that way of choreographing, in order to dance or give yourself the parts you always wanted, has disappeared a little bit.

Q: What were some of the major challenges that you faced along your journey? Were there difficult choices that you had to make? Are there ones you might have made differently in retrospect?

DJ: There were difficult ones, because once I left that one company that demanded my body and soul twenty-four hours a day, it was very hard to make a reasonable schedule. Many companies had only one performance a year in New York. So, as a dancer trying to make ends meet, I'd be working with three or four different people. I worked for a while doing occasional touring with a small ballet company, John Begg's Ballet Carnival, that did children's shows. I was the narrator (a clown), and I also toured with a small company called Mara and Her Legends of Cambodia. I picked up the style as best I could and handled the stage managing in addition to dancing.

Q: That's funny!

DJ: Uh huh! [*laughs*]

Q: And I take it that Mara was dancing her own solos?

DJ: Mara? Well, she featured herself in three kinds of choreography: an adult concert show, a children's concert show, and a solo nightclub act. And they all had basically the same choreography [*laughing*], but the slant was different. We others were Cha'o Li Chi, who was a Chinese—well, we called them shadow boxers then...I guess he did a sort of tai chi—and Edna Evans, who had studied Kathakali[2] in India, and Mara, who was born in Manchuria of

Russian and French parentage and who had studied in Jakarta and Pnom Penh and knew all these Asian forms. She had also studied composition with Doris Humphrey. So the four of us toured, and when we did the children's shows, we had a beautiful little girl, a Eurasian girl, who did the lead. So, in trying to balance Mara's little tour dates and the ballet company's tour dates and performing with Mary Anthony and performing with so-and-so here and so-and-so there, sometimes I ended up seriously inconveniencing someone or damaging my standing with one person because of some performance another had.

I think probably the most painful decision was…while I was a member of Juilliard Dance Theater, I had been in José Limón's *Missa Brevis* at the premiere and I had been taking classes at his studio. I don't think I was dancing wonderfully because I had had a knee operation and I hadn't recovered very well from it. But I was taking his classes. They were in the early evening. And I knew he was taking an extended company to do *Missa* and Doris Humphrey's *Passacaglia* as part of his South American tour. But suddenly I had no more money. And I was babysitting for a living. So I said to somebody like Betty Jones or Ruth Currier, "I can't come to class anymore, please tell José…"

And so, I didn't get asked to go on that tour. Apparently, somebody else who had been in the original cast of *Missa* said to him, "Why not *me*?" And he said, "Well, you didn't come to class." So I felt really bad, like something had changed for me. If I had gone on that tour, who knows, my career might have taken some slightly different turn. I don't know. I certainly would have seen an interesting part of the world.

There were other things along the way I didn't get because I was too tall or something. I mean I remember auditioning for Paul Taylor once when there were only five people auditioning. And he said to me [*laughs*] in his sort of faux-hick way, "You're lookin' real good, but I need an itty bitty girl." [*laughs*] He ended up taking a medium-sized person. But anyway, so yes, of course one encounters things like that.

I don't think I had any completely heartbreaking setbacks, just some disappointments, some sense of being in the wrong place at the wrong time and not being in the right place at the right time. Or having to juggle my schedule so much that I couldn't do it all and lost out on some things. And you know in retrospect, it is very easy to say, "Why didn't I study with Merce Cunningham?" I might have starved, but look at what an amazing venture I would have been in on! Or, "Gee, I could have taken Bob Dunn's[3] classes," but I don't think I would have understood them at that time.

Q: You mentioned the juggling. This is such a theme with almost any dancer I've ever met. We are such amazing jugglers of time. Did you find the juggling between this and that part of your dance life harder and harder to do? Did it get harder to switch hats between performing, choreographing, writing—even though it's all dance?

DJ: I don't feel it was so hard to switch hats. Things were different then. When I started studying modern dance, we didn't think so much about technical expertise. You know, we thought about being a wonderful dancer. We didn't think about being able to stand on one leg for a certain amount of time or the number of turns we could take. We thought about how to make the movement look luscious. And I was always a very good performer, before I had any technique to speak of.

I remember I was taking classes briefly at May O'Donnell's studio, and I was amazed at the dancers like Gertrude Shurr! I mean these women…they had muscles! I didn't have muscles like that! They were on the floor and they were doing all these things, with their little bare legs and all…And I thought, "Oh my God!" You know!

[*laughter*]

And I mean I loved May's classes. Gertrude Shurr's classes were rigorous in a different way, but I remember saying to Gertrude, "Um, Charles Weidman has asked me to perform with him," and her looking at me and saying, "Well, Debbie," which is what people called me then, "Well, Debbie, you know, as far as I'm concerned, you are nowhere near ready to appear on the stage."

Deborah Jowitt dancing in her own choreography at the 92nd Street YMCA.

Well, I had never thought that! And I started getting that from other people, too, like…*technique*…all of a sudden *technique*! At some point, I was studying at the Graham School, which, of course, was fairly rigorous, and suddenly somebody said to me, "You know, you really should go back to ballet." And so, I went to the Joffrey School, and at first I thought, "My God! Am I supposed to be able to do all this?" It was pretty late for me to be thinking that way! You know?

But, I didn't have this "I've got to take class every day or my legs will fall off." I would take class maybe three times a week. I liked class, but not like some people who devotedly slaved away in class after class. And choreography was fun. At DTW [Dance Theater Workshop], I would be choreographing something and dancing in somebody else's piece, and that was fine. I mean, it was very relaxing to put aside that aspect of creativity and just perform, to try to be there and serve the choreographer.

When I started to write, I was still so involved in doing all these other things that it was…well, I wrote in a somewhat different way then; the writing was maybe a little more colloquial, a little bit more from the inside. And I thought at first that it would involve more of a separation from performing and choreographing, but then I decided it couldn't. I was already too involved. I already knew too many people. I was writing about people I knew.

Q: Was that tricky for you at first? Is it still tricky?

DJ: Well, it's different now. I mean *then* they were all my peers. They were my colleagues. And I would sometimes have to say so. I even wrote something about Jeff Duncan after a concert I was *in* (explaining that I had been in it and this is what his style seemed to me to be like). And the dance community was extremely understanding. That is, the dancers were. They liked that I had a track record, that I was one of them, that I wasn't coming from the outside. They thought that was fine.

Some of the writers didn't approve. I remember Doris Hering reviewed a piece that I had made. She didn't like the piece and wrote that if I couldn't be a better choreographer I should stop, because otherwise people would stop trusting me as a writer. As if somehow…if I were a great choreographer, that would be okay. But if I were only a mediocre choreographer, then somehow that would damage my credentials as a writer.

I thought about that, but I rejected it. And my choreography did get better. Beginning in the early seventies maybe, I did some really nice pieces. But none of the dancers or choreographers seemed to think, "Well, she's not so good. How does she get off criticizing me?" If they said that privately, I don't know about it, but they certainly never gave me that impression. It was like when I was writing, I was writing. And when I was a choreographer, I was a choreographer. That was fine. You know, I did what I could do.

Now the situation is a bit different. There's so much dance going on. And I know the people involved in a different way. I don't just know my peers; there are also my former students to consider. I mean, how many years do I have to wait after they graduate before I can write about their performances? But somehow I seem to be able to keep my head above water.

Q: What are some of the major ideas you would want to relate to dancers struggling to survive in the dance world?

DJ: To dancers? Not choreographers? But just to dancers?

Q: Well, to dancers, choreographers, writers…all of them. What would you like to tell them?

DJ: Well, I don't know. The thing is that there are so many people giving advice that anything you say just sounds like a rehash of Linda Hamilton's column in *Dance Magazine*. You know, what to do about your weight and how not to become anorexic, and what to do about injuries…

Q: But what about the inner self?

DJ: Well, the inner self is so affected by those outer things. And there's different kinds of advice you would give to somebody who is in a major company and somebody who is in a small studio, hoping to become a professional dancer. I've been a participant in a couple of conferences held at The Hague, the first of which was done jointly with a conference in Toronto via satellite link. It was called "Not Just Any Body." And the second one was called "Not Just Any Body and Soul." In workshops and panels, there was extremely progressive thinking about the body and how to hold it together, and how to think about it, and how to train it. There was a great deal of talk, in particular during the last one, about how dance can lead to unhealthy behavior, mentally as well as physically. For example, allowing oneself to be dominated, to be completely submissive to a choreographer or company director. And the whole thrust of the conferences was to make dancers become more empowered within the dance community. To find ways to make their voices heard within the work situation. Obviously, in a rehearsal, the choreographer is the boss and you do whatever he or she says. But that can be a very unhealthy spiritual, mental, and physical lifestyle if you're not careful.

And there are all sorts of movements afoot. Some dancers, most of them from the Merce Cunningham Company, have begun to circulate online something called "The Dancers' Compact." And it includes sorts of things like how many hours you can rehearse, how to deal with your opinion being solicited from the choreographer, health care…

I think that the dancer's struggle is to keep sight of whatever his or her goal is and to make sure it is a sensible, reasonable goal. Not, say, trying to be a ballerina if you have a body that is not acceptable in today's kinds of companies. You have to have a realistic goal, but also an ambitious one that challenges you. And you have to love what you're doing and have a clear understanding of why you're doing it. That it's not out of vanity, or to satisfy your parents, or to live up to somebody else's idea of you. But that you are doing it because the dancing itself is something that you love. And you keep yourself healthy in every way in order to do it. These are not unusual ideas.

Q: And for dance writers? What do you think about the dance writing field now?

DJ: I think that dance has suffered in the past by not having a body of scholarship in the way, say, the visual arts do, or film. Years ago, there weren't that many dance books. Now there are dance books being published all the time by university presses and mainstream presses. And there's a push toward an intense dance scholarship that's building on French literary theory, Marxist theory, feminist theory, queer theory…There's a need to prove that dance can hold its own in this scholarly domain. The language can be abstruse, but it's great that we have provocative thinking focusing on dance. The more dance books there are, and books written by dancer-choreographers, too, like Ralph Lemon's *Geography*…well, it's beautiful. *That* is just a *beautiful* book. So the outpouring of serious books on dance is comparatively recent. As far as writing dance criticism, that's different.

Q: How so?

DJ: If you've got a good book, you can find a publisher somehow. They may not pay you much, but you can get it published. Not necessarily so with dance criticism. But that situation is changing, too. People have had to struggle to find a print venue, whether that meant writing for a little neighborhood paper, or covering New York events for, say, a British dance magazine. And there are a lot of people scrambling for very few jobs, many of which pay little or nothing.

But now, there are all these online publications. I mean, there is Paul Ben-Itzak's Web site Dance Insider.com; there is the online version of Alexandra Tomalonis's *Dance View*. There are many people writing for them and writing very long reviews. There's no space limitation. And important critics who no longer have a print venue (and some who do), as well as many younger critics, are writing for those publications.

Q: But, on the other hand, you have, for example, the *Village Voice*, which has cut down on its dance coverage.

DJ: Well, the *Village Voice* is another problem.

Q: Even the *New York Times* has cut back on dance.

DJ: Yes, I hear that the *New York Times* now has some problems. But we [at the *Village Voice*] began to have a problem when Don Horst took over as editor and dance went from having a page and a half to having just a page and sometimes only half a page.

Q: Yes, I remember that it was a sad day.

DJ: Right. And in the last few months, since the fall I guess, we've had a redesign that is extremely rigid. In the 1980s, I could have the equivalent of a whole page if I wanted it, 1,600 words, and other writers were featured in the additional half page. The new redesign mandates that the lead review on any of the arts pages be around 900 words and that there be three other very short pieces. And so I usually have 900 words to cover two events. There's another possible layout in which I write 600 words about *one* thing and more short pieces appear.

Q: Wow.

DJ: And, of course, the editors hope I'll review something that's still running, which is almost never possible.

Q: And do you get to choose what you want to look at and write about?

DJ: Pretty much. In collaboration with the dance editor, Elizabeth Zimmer, of course. But that was always true. I was spoiled when Burt Supree was the dance editor and we had a page and a half and I would regularly write features. In fact, my contract said that I had to do at least four in-depth looks at a certain choreographer or phenomenon a year. The paper doesn't want that kind of feature anymore. I've written some features for the front of the paper, but they can always be bumped to the back of the book, where they may preempt the review space. So I got a little discouraged from doing them. The heyday of dance at the *Voice* seems to be gone.

Q: And now as both a writer and as a critic, is all this sort of self-motivated? Do you capture an idea in your head and think, "Oh, maybe I can sell that!"

DJ: Yes, or some really competent press agent like Ellen Jacobs calls me up and says, you know, "Robert Rauschenberg is collaborating with Trisha Brown on a new work. Will you think about that as a story?" There are not many press agents who are that creative, but sometimes it works that way, or an editor at another publication will approach me about an article. A feature is usually tied to an upcoming event, not just hatched in left field.

There's another thing about the business of dance. I am very lucky because I do have health insurance.

Q: Through the *Voice*?

DJ: Yes. So if I were to stop writing for the *Voice*, with the exception of getting Medicare, I would have to pay for health insurance myself. So I try to roll with the punches. That's the practical side of it all.

Q: Are you seeing any significant trends that you've noticed in any aspect of the dance field, either in training or the attitudes of people both in or out of the field, or in the subject matter that is being explored more?

DJ: Well, I implied before that I think training has become more humane. You know, you don't see as many weighing machines in the hallways of studios and schools.

Q: Boy, do I remember those! [*laughs*]

DJ: We had one at NYU in the halls when I was first teaching there, and then one day somebody put a sign on it, saying, "For Faculty Only." I thought that was a good way to get rid of it! [*laughs*] But, no, it's a little more humane, and even the New York City Ballet dancers who go to West Side Dance Physical Therapy get bone density tests, which may help somebody to probe their dieting problems. I think dancers are just a lot more conscious of their bodies and how to manage them than they were when I started in dance.

As for choreography, it's sort of hard to spot trends when you are in the middle of them. But it does seem significant to me that in contemporary dance, we went through a period when the important things were movement and form. You know, the best thing to do was to be able to create new systems of movement and new structures. Merce Cunningham and George Balanchine were exemplars of that plotless approach. And in the work of the Judson Dance Theater people, narrative was taboo. In the sixties, Meredith Monk was maybe one of the few—and Kenneth King to some degree—who pursued drama and narrative in their work. But in very contemporary ways, in tune with the times. Then somewhere around the late seventies, there began to be a new interest in narrative and emotion. It was around the time that painting began to realign itself around figurative stuff. I think that we have seen a steady growth in dance theater. Pina Bausch, her visits, have had a strong influence. But an influence not in terms of copying her, which is what some of the Germans did, but in terms of the freedom to tackle emotion again. Some choreographers have said to me, "You know, it was liberating to see that you could deal with narrative and character but not in an old-fashioned way." So I think we're still in that era of dance theater, but other elements are coming in. For instance, there is a lot of interest in popular culture. In hip-hop, in club dancing, etc...I'm thinking of another generation, people like David Neumann, Doug Elkins, Nicholas Leichter, and there are a lot of others who sort of use popular culture in their movement style. I saw a piece at DTW about Britney Spears called *Britney's Inferno*. It was choreographed by Headlong Dance Theater, and it was very, very funny. A very elaborate spoof of popular culture.

Q: And you're continuing to choreograph?

DJ: Well, now I choreograph only for the NYU students. I make a piece in the fall for the Faculty Performance Workshop using first-year or second-year students, or first-year MFAs.

Q: And what themes are interesting you? If you were to take a look at the past three or four pieces you've done?

DJ: Well, I think my pieces are all about basically the same thing: groups and how individuals function within groups, but in a non-narrative structure. That's been my main interest in choreography.

Q: And do you have any personal wishes or hopes for the dance field? Or do you want to simply see what happens?

DJ: I don't like to make predictions. There are all kinds of things that one could hope for, like an increase in government subsidies. But dancers are endlessly inventive when these dry up. Some companies fold. Still, people find ways of working. Theaters close, and they find new ones. They're incredibly resourceful and hardy. The big ballet companies have other, much more severe financial problems because they have more of an establishment to maintain. I hate to see them grappling and groping to find what they think will be popular with the audiences. You know, choose some hot, new something-or-other. American Ballet Theatre occasionally puts its foot in its mouth with these choices. But the need to attract a public is oppressive for some of the big companies.

Q: And what keeps you going? What drives you and gets you excited?

DJ: About dance performances?

Q: Yes, about dance performances and about what you do? What do you love about it?

DJ: Well, I always hope that I'll see something that will be wonderful and marvelous. Or thrilling in terms of being new or different from what I've seen before. It can even be distasteful but provocative…and also, reading about dance, writing about dance, talking with colleagues, there's always something. To read new ideas about dancing, a stimulating thought about it in some new book…or to read a review by somebody—a really good writer—and be amazed all over again at the power that words can have used skillfully. I cry when I read really beautiful dance writing.

NOTES

1. Judson Dance Theater was a collective of choreographers, composers, and visual artists who frequently performed together at the Judson Memorial Church in Greenwich Village, NY, in the 1960s. Their avant-garde manifesto, a rejection of Western theatrical dance forms and movement techniques, gave rise to postmodern dance. Original members of the group included Lucinda Childs, Yvonne Rainer, Steve Paxton, David Gordon, and Trisha Brown.

2. Kathakali, one of the major classical dance–drama forms of India, originally developed as a popular form in Kerala, on the southwest coast of India in the sixteenth century. Like other Southeast Asian dance and theater forms, the repertory is based on stories from the ancient Sanskrit epics the *Mahabharata* and the *Ramayana*. Kathakali performances often begin at dusk and last until dawn. They are noted for their generally all-male casts, vigorous highly stylized movements, elaborate costumes, headdresses, and makeup.

3. Robert Ellis Dunn (1929–1967) was a composer and choreographer who worked as an accompanist for many modern dance choreographers including Merce Cunningham. Dunn began teaching dance composition classes at the invitation of John Cage, Cunningham's long-time musical director, and eventually transferred his classes to Judson Memorial Church, where he became a guiding figure in the postmodern dance movement.

Carolyn Carlson

CAROLYN CARLSON

"It's like a meditation. The curtain opens and you have to be there and it's only this moment, now."

California-born Carolyn Carlson received her early dance training at the San Francisco School of Ballet and the University of Utah. After dancing as a lead soloist for Alwin Nikolais between 1965 and 1970, Carlson began working in Paris and gradually found her artistic home in Europe. Since moving to Europe over thirty-five years ago, Carlson has influenced countless European artists through her work as a choreographer and/or artistic director for such institutions as the Paris Opera Research Group (Groupe de Recherches Théâtrales: GRTOP); Théâtre de la Ville, Paris; the Teatro la Fenice, Venice; the Venice Biennale; the Culberg Ballet, Stockholm; and for many other companies throughout Europe. Since 2002, with the support of the city of Paris, Carlson has directed Atelier de Paris-Carolyn Carlson, her creative base and a dance center offering master classes and workshops conducted by both emerging and well-known artists, such as Jennifer Muller, Trisha Brown, Susanne Linke, Ushio Amagatsu, Bill T. Jones, Wim Vandekeybus, Michele Anne de Mey, Marie Chouinard, and others. Carlson's numerous awards include Prize for Best Dancer, Paris International Dance Festival (1968); the Victoires de la Musique prize for *Signes* (1998); the title of Chevalier des Arts et Lettres; the award of Chevalier de la Legion d'Honneur by the president of the French Republic (2000); and La Medaille de la Ville de Paris (2002). Her collection of poetry, entitled *Solo*, was published in 2003.

SETTING THE SCENE

During my years of teaching and performing in Europe in the 1990s, there were a few American artists whose name, work, and reputation would often greet me in the studios where I visited. Carolyn was one of these artists. A visit to her atelier in the eastern outskirts of Paris was like a visit to the Zen gardens that inspire her. Housed within a magnificent park, Carolyn's atelier is a simple dance oasis: one studio and modest offices; an alternative nursery school next door; an avant-garde theater and café across the courtyard. My New York sensibility, used to cramped quarters and noisy streets, envied the utopian conditions. But, as our conversation revealed, this was a hard-won simplicity, sought after by a statuesque, energetic Californian, who at any moment seems ready to pull up stakes and set out for further adventures. Our effervescent visit together was like a glass of champagne at noon.

— R.C.

Q: The first question I have for you is, if you were in a group of children, perhaps the children next door, or a group of nondancers, how would you describe your work? Or even with dancers, what do you say you do?

CC: What a question! I never really describe what I do, because as soon as I describe it, it disappears. The writer Rilke said that if you try to explain your work, what you say is not what it is. I don't really speak about my work. Choreographing is *my* way of speaking. I'm really about action. It's through the teaching, the doing that people understand. I just completed a second book of poetry. I think by reading my books of poetry, you understand who I am because it connects to this intangible kind of energy force, and that's what dance is about.

Q: Do you consider your involvement with dance to be your profession? Is it your career, your work, your passion, your calling, or is it all of the above?

CC: Well, there are no boxes for me. I mean, it's my life. I feel very blessed. I teach. I still perform. I choreograph. I direct festivals. I write. I care.

Q: And as a performer, if you could say something about that, as it has evolved for you.

CC: Oh, it's amazing. I've always been fascinated by the nature of performance. To me, what is so fascinating about dance is that it involves a real risk in life. The curtain opens and you've got to do it right now. You can't close the curtain and say, "I'm sorry. I can't perform tonight." It's like a meditation. The curtain opens and you have to be there and it's only this moment, now.

Q: Has your relationship to performing changed as you've matured?

CC: Oh yes, I've taken more risk the older I am. For example, I took a risk in one of my recent solos, *Writings on Water*. It's a very

Zen piece, based on the tea ceremony, performed in a black skirt, something like the man's traditional costume for Kabuki,[1] with a very low Japanese table for a set. I start with my head bowed, and slowly I raise it. Nothing more. Simple.

But, what is so incredible about dance, and this is what I was saying to my dancers at the performance you saw last night, "I don't care if you're not together. I want you to shine. You get out there and you be generous." What I love about performing is the act of giving. You're throwing energy out. It's like a conversation. You throw those gestures out and you are received. And you can tell, especially in a solo, you can sense the conversation between you and the audience. When I first started working with the dancers at the opera, they thought I was crazy. We were there on stage, throwing gestures out in space and I said, "I want you guys to break that sound barrier." And I mean, the Bastille Opera is a killer. The size is like an airport.

Q: Yes. I was wondering about the challenges of translating modern dance to such large halls like you have here in Europe.

CC: Well, it's incredible and full of challenges. So, I said, "Okay, you guys, I want you to turn and I want you to *hurl* your chest all the way to the back rows." And they came away from that experience and said, "We understand something differently now!" That was great, because, in the ballet, you work the body…but in my work, we work with space and time and soul energy. People usually say the soul is in the body, but for me, the soul is out there. And we're filling, we're reaching, we're going out to it. And this is what I teach. So the dancers come away having had a mind-opening experience. Instead of standing up vertically, they stand up between the heaven and the earth. This thinking comes from tai chi. Dance for me is like a spiritual exercise of connecting with the universe of forces. This is *my* work.

Q: How did you first get introduced to dance and what have been some of the landmark events in your dance life? Who were and are some of the major influences and inspirations in your life?

CC: Alwin Nikolais. Alwin Nikolais was definitely the major influence in my life. I grew up in Fresno, California, and had taken classes there and in San Francisco. When I was fifteen, I entered an amateur contest. And you know, I was just meeting the boys then. I had this little tutu, I don't know, I think I was a canary with these feathers and toe shoes. [*laughter*] I was already pretty tall. I tell you, I was laughed off the stage, really laughed off the stage. And so, I put my toe shoes away. I didn't dance again until I was nineteen. Instead, I was a pom-pom girl, and part of my generation in California was cars and drive-ins and the sixties stuff. And then I went to the University of Utah, where I heard they had a very fine modern dance department. I was disillusioned by ballet, so I majored in philosophy and poetry. On the side, I was taking modern dance classes. And Joan Woodbury was teaching there, and she said, "You must take a workshop with Nikolais." I said, "Who's that?" She said, "Alwin Nikolais." And I'll never forget it. I took one class from him and it was like…[*pause*] I felt this huge door opening that I have never closed since. It was an incredible, intense workshop. He worked on concepts in the abstractions of time, space, shape, motion, and transformation. He has been a major influence in my work as a performer and choreographer. I danced with Nikolais for seven years, and during this time, I was beginning to do my own choreographies, as he encouraged us to reach out and experience our own unique gestures. He made us all very creative. So, eventually, I wanted and *needed* to leave. In 1971, we were touring in Paris with the Nikolais company, when I saw a performance of Robert Wilson's *Deaf Man's Glance*. I was astounded by his work, and he inspired me to go in another direction. Robert Wilson became a major influence for me. For me, he still is my hero. His lights, his design, his severity. His concepts. Years later, in 1997, he saw my ballet *Signes* at the Opera de Bastille. He gave me a "chapeau"[2] after the show. I was honored to learn that we were in mutual admiration of each other's work.

Q: And you mentioned that tai chi is influencing you also?

CC: In New York, I discovered Zen Buddhism. Sitting meditation and calligraphy. New York changed my life. I think the thinking is deeper on the East Coast from my California hippie generation. I really loved the West, the sun the openness and everything, but it's not the same philosophical approach to art.

Q: What were some of the major challenges you faced along your journey to this point and what are some of the choices you had to make? Were there difficult choices? Are there choices that stand out as exceptionally good ones? Are there choices in retrospect that you might have made differently? I mean, coming to Europe was a choice.

CC: Coming to Europe was a milestone. In 1973, Rolf Liebermann, director of the Paris Opera, invited me to do a solo at the Paris Opera, later the creation *Density 21.5* with music by Edgard Varèse. It was a revolution. Everyone in France was saying, "Who's this? A bird in a gilded cage—a great success as the technique was joined with a strong poetics." After this adventure, Liebermann asked me to stay and create a new work for the Paris Opera with John Davis. We were ready to go back to New York to start our own company but John said, "With an opportunity like this, we're staying in Europe."

Q: You had left Alwin by this time?

CC: Yes, I had already left in 1970. I kind of forget these memories, but as I recall, John and I were floating between London and Germany for about a year. We were just getting ready to go back to America, and then the most amazing thing happened. At the last minute, Liebermann said, "Start a group here." I mean, the Paris Opera was the biggest name in town! I said, "I'm not so sure with these dancers." But, we tried. So, the first day down in the rotonde at the Paris Opera, I had thirty people for class. The second day I had ten; the third day I had three. And, you know, I tried to tell them to stand up. They were like this [*mimicking a stiff stance*]. I said, "No, no, no, keep your head on your spine with grace, no tension,

40

think Zen." And they were saying, "Who is this lady? We don't accept her concepts." And then dear Liebermann said, "It's okay. Open the doors to other dancers outside of the opera!" In order to form a new company later to become the GRTOP (Groupe de Recherches Théâtrales), Liebermann granted me the title of *étoile*, star of the Paris Opera. So I opened the doors in our new studio, La Rotonde, and it was a revolution in dance training in France. I was teaching technique, composition, and improvisation. By the end of two months, we had young dancers throughout Europe coming, and everyone in the dance community knew something was happening. It was a fantastic experience for the French dancers because up to this point, artists were always coming and going. Merce Cunningham had been here. Maurice Béjart had been here as well as Alwin Nikolais. But I was one of the first choreographers to stay and inspire this young generation.

The ballet dancers in the beginning rebelled against my installation at the opera, which was understandable. In 1980, five years later, they accepted my work, which included *Slow, Heavy and Blue* for the Paris Opera company. Under the GRTOP, we received boos and bravos. One example was *Il y a juste un instant* [There is just an Instant] where Barre Philipps, the bass player, came on stage with bare feet and long hair down to his waist, wearing a long Indian robe and playing very contemporary strange music. And Larrio Ekson, my partner, and I were doing unusual fast motion sequences, and I was dancing like a broken bird. Then somebody yelled, "This is a cabaret, a cabaret!" and all the public was divided. You know, just screaming and disagreeing with each other. And Rolf Liebermann said, "Darling, I love it, keep it going." So, this was another turning point for my career. The critics were talking about the work as well as the performance and the teaching methods, which had gathered a successful momentum. After this experience, John Davis and I were planning to go back to New York again, and John said, "With a chance like *this*, we're staying in Paris!"

Q: And John was also a performer?

CC: No, he was a lighting designer. We came here together and he spoke French immediately. We were together eight years and he created all my lights for each production in France. John also created his own revolution, with his brilliant stage and lighting design. Everyone was amazed with the magic he created on stage, a space of poetry and genius.

Q: What do you think you were bringing from your tradition here? Was it the improvisational techniques from Nik?

CC: Well, it's hard to say. But the people here say that I gave them *a way*. Because when they improvised and did their own compositions, they could believe in themselves. I worked with the concepts of Alwin Nikolais and Gaston Bachelard.[3] Working with time, time as memory, time moving forward, time stopping, space as enclosures and voids, we generated a new thinking concerning the art of dance. With these enormous concepts, we progressed each day. And it gave the dancers a chance to be inventive and discover their own way. Europe has a very old history and development, and because of that, the thinking is more…rational and Cartesian, in comparison to the spontaneity of America.

Q: And what *was* here before you first arrived?

CC: Maurice Béjart created his own revolution in the early fifties. His ballets had a psychological drama inherent in the story line. He had an enormous popularity with a large public. And then there was Félix Blaska, who was choreographing for his modern company on an experimental level. Merce Cunningham and Alwin Nikolais arrived in the sixties and seventies to perform and both made major breakthroughs in the vision of dance. In Germany, dance expressionism had its connection to the histories of Rudolf Laban, Mary Wigman, Dalcroze, and Kurt Jooss. But in France, ballet still had a very strong influence at that time.

Q: Any other choices that you recall? Like when you met Nikolais, then you said you must go to New York. That was an obvious one.

CC: Yes. I was with Nik for seven years, and since his teaching was about choreography, I felt this necessity to go out on my own, as he engendered our creativity. I love Nikolais's work, but I had something else inside of me. When we were touring in Paris in 1968, the strangest thing happened to me, déjà vu. I think everybody has these moments. On a free night, we went to see a performance of Robert Wilson's *Five Hours of Slow Motion*. During the performance, I turned to John and said, "John, I think we're going to leave Nik. This is too much for me." I mean, I got so inspired. And then the next day, we were walking down the avenue de l'Opéra, and I was looking at the opera house, never in a thousand, million years thinking that we would work *there*, and I said, "John, I have a feeling we're going to move here." Just like that. Then we went back to New York and everything changed.

Telling Nik that I wanted to leave was the hardest thing that I ever had to do because Nikolais was a father figure, and my master. As I told him that I had to leave, he looked at me, with tears in his eyes, and he said, "No one is irreplaceable." We had always had a very good rapport because as a dancer I could execute whatever he wanted. So, that was one *whammo* over the head. And then he added, "There's no democracy in art." This, I'll never forget, which I still say today. There is something about the dance world that makes it a hell of a living. I'm blessed. I'm sixty and I'm still moving around. But there are times, especially as a dancer, you know, we have injuries, or at a certain age, you have to stop or you can't find work. I think dance is one of the most difficult professions. A pianist can sit down, eat a lot, a painter works in solitude, and a filmmaker has his eyes behind the camera, but a dancer has to be there 99 percent.

Q: What made you leave Nikolais?

CC: I wanted to do my own work. I had to leave. I didn't know what I was going to do. John and I tried to get money in New York; we did a few small shows. But nobody would support us. Everybody said, "Do something." I said, "I can't do something if I have to pay my people." Then, I had an opportunity to teach in the London Contemporary School, Martha Graham's school, in 1970. And then

I was floating around teaching in Germany and in Paris. In Paris, I was contacted by Anne Beranger. She had a small company, for which I was commissioned to create three new works. That's when I met Maurice Béjart and all these great musicians, John Surman, Barre Philipps, Michel Portal, Dieter Fleichtner, all of whom I worked with later. Anne was a great lady and patron of the arts in the Paris circle. She didn't dance herself, but she had the ability to get unique artists together and also to get money.

Q: And you felt that you found support here that you didn't find in the States?

CC: Well…it just happened. Because we tried in New York. Maybe if I had returned…but I didn't…you know, it snowballed here. My first contact was with Anne Beranger and Rolf Liebermann at the Paris Opera. Working with Anne was my first experience in France, and John and I were amazed. I would be teaching the company and she would usually come during the middle of class. A very beautiful lady. Very small, petite. Red hair standing in long curls. She always had her little eucalyptus cigarettes with her. The class would stop and everyone would come up and kiss her. Well, you know, I'm American, you *do the class*. Even to this day, you know, when people want to kiss me after the show, I don't know, it's very difficult for me.

So, the way people behaved here was a huge revelation for John and me. But there was something about Europeans. I must say, in France, they fell in love with my work from the beginning. My work is physical and esoteric. It deals with nonlinear connotations, meaning, "There's no story, it's more like a poem." And, like poetry, you have something to hold on to that is not necessarily coherent in a rational way. I mean, you have a beginning, a middle, and an end—but it's not a novel. So, I think this mysticism and dreamlike reality fascinated the French people. I don't know if I could have done this in New York. The one person in America I feel close to artistically is Martha Clarke. We worked together years ago and we have a strong liaison.

After working at the opera from 1974 to 1980, Maestro Italo Gomez from Italy asked me to create the same dance experience for the artists at Teatro la Fenice in Venice for four years. I built a very strong group there and the same thing happened: we caused a revolution in Italy.

I formed a company of seven Italian dancers, and it shocked the public as they weren't used to the Italians doing contemporary dance. But the results were overwhelmingly positive, and we won the Italian hearts. These dancers are all well-known choreographers now. I'm very proud of that.

In 1979, I met René Aubry, a great musician and composer. We've done about twenty creations together. We had a child in Venice and then we came back to Paris and worked with Gérard Violette at Théâtre de la Ville in Paris, and the company toured in Italy, Switzerland, Spain, Finland, and France. Then I was invited to work in Finland at the Helsinki City Theater for two years.

In France, the support for the arts is substantial. In America, with Nikolais, we were performing in university theaters. I would like to go back to New York but what's in?

Q: What does that mean?

CC: I don't know, what's in? You know, people strip on stage these days. Maybe they want something like people going through glass and breaking their bodies on the floor. But my work is my work. It's not like that. I'm fine in Europe. It's kind of too bad being American and never working there. But you know, I think there's a certain kind of destiny. Both my grandparents are from Finland and my parents are first generation American, it's like I'm close to home, living in France. In my deep center I will always remain American, but my work has been inspired by living in Europe. My dancers are mostly European from France, Italy, and Finland; they are organic, round, and sensual.

Q: You came home, in a way. What are the Finnish dancers like?

CC: Oh, they're fantastic, incredible, incredible! The Finnish mentality is absolutely crazy. I love working with these people. They are totally out. Tero Saarinen and Jorma Uotinen are two great choreographers whom I've worked with. These people are crazy. You tell them to do something, and they just do it. You tell them to jump out the window; they jump out the window. They have this mind that's creative in an absurd way, perhaps because Finland is so isolated in the North. I lived there for two years and, I mean, in November, December, January, February, it's dark at three o'clock. It's dark at three o'clock in the afternoon. Personally, I liked it because I found myself in this mystic space. In the summer, the sun never goes down, so there's something captivating about the isolation of color and light. The high stars from the North: it makes people changeable and unique.

Q: What are some of the major ideas that you would want to relate to dancers struggling to survive and thrive in the dance world? What would you like to tell them?

CC: Go ahead and carry on. That's the most difficult. I have tears here. We have auditions at the Atelier; we have tears all the time. "How come you didn't take me?" It's very difficult. I think you just have to persist and believe in your self-image. And if you have a will, you will make it. You just have to go in and do the best you can, and don't be dejected if you're not taken; life has many roads. But I think young dancers forget that you can just have a great time doing a class, without the preoccupation if you're accepted or not accepted. Enjoy dancing. That's how it used to be. But now there's so much pressure. "How come I'm not in a company? Why didn't I get in this?" Acceptance of defeat is a gift. I don't know what it's like in America now, but in Europe it's very difficult.

Q: It's extremely difficult there as well. [*pause*] So, what's the hardest thing for you?

CC: The funding of a project. I'm now director of the Centre Chorégraphique in Roubaix, where we have wonderful studios, a theater to perform in, as well as opportunities for touring in Europe and the Far East. However, we must still have sponsorships from the government and other theaters.

Q: And having a full company here would tie you down?

CC: I have a wonderful organization in Roubaix with assistants, and I don't always tour with the company as I also write poetry books and teach master classes, as well as creating works for other companies.

Q: And what about the training of your company, when you do need them? In New York, dancers are taking things like Pilates and yoga, but they seem to be taking fewer classic modern dance classes, where people are moving together within a structure on a routine basis. Do you find that here?

CC: That's why we give intensive workshops here taught by masters at the Atelier de Paris. We have had a great Nikolais workshop, as well as classes by Wim Vandekeybus, Marie Chouinard, and Joseph Nadj, for example. It's important to preserve the traditions of masters teaching the younger generations, on a one-to-one exchange.

Q: And developing the work in the class.

CC: Dance is experiencing motion, whatever choice of master you desire to follow.

Q: Do you see any significant trends in any aspect of the dance field? Either in training or in the attitude of people, both in and out of the field. In subject matter? What do you think is going on?

CC: I find it's unfortunate now that a lot of choreographers don't teach. To teach is to understand the language of the choreographer. Anne Teresa de Keersmaeker has made a great step starting her school in Brussels. She has a strong technique, very musical, and composition classes, and consequently she's producing a talented line of dancers.

I think it's so wise when a choreographer teaches. The dancers receive ideas through the basis of the work. That's my training from Nikolais. He did everything.

Q: And in the style of what you're seeing in the theaters. Is what the French audience wants changing?

CC: Well, again, I realize that my point of view is very special. I mean, I get terribly bored if I just see dance steps on stage. Even if the people are good. I see a lot of performances but I can't say I like them all. I know many producers like controversial work. What's amazing to me is that you can't shock people anymore. You cannot shock! I mean you have this naked guy, his balls flapping and everything. I mean, I find it so unaesthetic. It's distracting. Why don't you just wrap it up like the Japanese and then you can see him dance? So, there's a big trend of trying to shock and of trying to be *in*. But you can't do it anymore.

Then there's Marie Chouinard from Canada. She's fantastic. And there's Joseph Nadj from Hungary. He did a most incredible piece on Balthus.[4] It was poetry, an imaginative dream. So there are all kinds of good things happening and all kinds of ridiculous things going on. However, I accept and respect other ideologies. Today, my feeling is that too many dancers want to choreograph and think they can choreograph. Most musicians work with a band or orchestra and they never think of composing, they think of playing. But dancers, somehow, don't think that they can just dance. They think that when you dance, that you also have to choreograph and that's changing things to mediocrity.

You know, I have to tell you, I read in the *New York Times Book Review* about a book written by two ex-dancers. They slandered the dance by saying things like, "There used to be dancers and choreographers," as if no one is left. They only talked about Mark Morris and, I think, Merce Cunningham. They said, "Modern dance is dead. Contemporary dance is like a thing in the air that will not last. It's over."

Q: Well, how do you feel about that?

CC: I disagree totally. Because I think there's something so vital about contemporary dance, modern dance. You know, I think it's something so strong, especially now, the way that people move. So, I don't understand. Personally, I think the two authors might be frustrated. You know, I thought it was kind of strange. And then they talked about Mark Morris. I'm sorry, Mark Morris does almost neoclassical work. I sometimes even find Merce Cunningham almost classical. So, I thought it was kind of strange how they think that this next generation can't survive, that the public's going away and this art form will disappear. Well, I disagree, but, hey, I can only speak for myself. There's no way it's going to happen here because it's so well supported and documented. Maybe America's different.

Q: Well, it's evolving in the States. I think some people think that it's evolving into something else.

CC: Theatrical?

Q: It's gotten theatrical?

CC: On stage, there are many verbal texts and philosophical statements. But I suppose that's just the nature of contemporary modern thought. Everyone has their own viewpoint and can do what they want. I don't know. It's interesting because you now have your Belgian choreographers, your Germans, and you have your French and Italians. And they all have a different kind of stand.

Q: Okay, if you had to pick, say, three reasons why you are still in this field, what would they be? What is it about this dance life that keeps you going? What do you love about it?

CC: Well, it's my artistic expression. A painter paints. A dancer shares energy. I find this métier fascinating because, as I said before, there's always a risk. It's like life and death. Martha Graham said, "I didn't choose dance, dance chose me." It's my karma. Oftentimes

Park, *choreographed and danced by Carolyn Carlson*

I feel that I've been a dancer before in another life. It sounds like Moira Shearer in *The Red Shoes*, right? [*laughter*]

Q: Stay away from trains!

CC: No, but it's true. My life has been blessed with great men supporting me. John Davis, lighting designer, René Aubry, composer, Thomas Erdos, impresario, Rolf Liebermann, Italo Gomez, theater director. My life has been totally filled with artists. Everything I see, I taste, I smell is full of art. And my son, he's now twenty-five and a great musician; he's already done two works for me. So, I have no categories for all of this. Believe me, I don't know what a *normal* life is anymore.

Q: And what are some of your visions, your dreams going forward from this point into the future?

CC: Besides master classes, I would like to open a professional school, which would be a four-year course as at the academy I had in Venice. It was fantastic. By the end of four years, we had people coming out of there as strong performers and choreographers. But, I left as director in 2002. Now we have a project going in Chiasso, Switzerland. It's a half hour from Milano. It's a huge, four-thousand-square-meter building that we found. It has something like five studios as big as this one. I mean, it's incredible. So it's the start of an academy there.

There are always projects between Roubaix and Paris. We have projects for film, a photo book, and two new creations planned for 2008.

Q: And all of these projects are coming to you? They're finding you?

CC: Yes, they find me and I find them. I kind of trust in the future. I never plan long range. I'm so spontaneous. My manager drives me crazy: "You must prepare, you must prepare for the future." But there's something in me that goes for the moment.

Q: You're in the moment.

CC: Zen and the continuance of Atelier de Paris.

Q: How long has it been here?

CC: Since 1999. I have to say this is one of the most beautiful parts of Paris, situated in a forest, green grass, horse stables, and facilities to initiate theater productions. Ariane Mnouchkine is the originator of the Théâtre du Soleil and the Cartoucherie space where we work.

Q: Yes, I can understand that. It's beautiful out here. Is there anything else, as far as communicating to an American audience that comes to your mind about what you're perceiving or wanting in your own work or in the dance world?

CC: There must be some kind of perception of beauty. The art of visual poetry never dies. I mean, you see a beautiful sunset, or you see the moon up there, and there's a moment, it's awesome. No matter what the idea is, I try to look for these clear pictures. And to be generous. Even if it's a very hard piece, as in *Dark* in 1998. It was based on the apocalypse, a strong subject. The pictures that I used from symbolic painters are today's scenes of silence and tragic circumstances. I will always keep to the heart line. And I still think people have a need for this. I think the human being needs love, however you want to define it. So this is a river running in my mind. It comes from my study of Zen. The Zen garden. How do you put fourteen rocks together? They're all different, yet there's a harmony and mystery.

NOTES

1. Kabuki, a classical Japanese dance theater form, originally developed as a popular form, often containing erotic content, performed by all female casts in Kyoto, in the sixteenth century. Since the mid-seventeenth century, all-male Kabuki casts perform a repertory of works based on history, folk tales, and even contemporary stories. Kabuki performances often lasting three hours or more are noted for their blend of dance, gesture, music, costume, makeup, and inventive stagecraft.

2. *Chapeau*, literally translated from French means "hat." To "give a chapeau" means "to tip one's hat to" and is a sign of congratulations and respect in French culture.

3. Gaston Bachelard (1888–1962) was a French philosopher whose work focused on the philosophy of science and knowledge, poetics, psychoanalysis, and the imagination.

4. Born Baltusz Klossowski de Rola in Paris, the painter known as Balthus (1908–2001) was entirely self-taught. Despite the fact that he used traditional painting techniques, his innovative approach to traditional subjects often gave his paintings a sense of menacing enigma. He is best known for paintings of adolescent girls and psychologically probing portraits, although he also painted landscapes, street scenes, and still lifes.

The Washington Post

Andrea Snyder

ANDREA SNYDER

"I dream that dance will step up among the cultural art forms as an equal to opera and theater and music and be attractive to people to come to and enjoy and understand and love and do."

Born and raised on Long Island, New York, Andrea Snyder is one of the leading advocates for dance in the United States. Snyder's early experiences in dance administration included work for the Dance Notation Bureau, the Cunningham Dance Foundation, the New York University Tisch School of the Arts Dance Department, Laura Dean Dancers and Musicians, and Sheldon Soffer Management. From 1987 to 1993, Snyder was an assistant director of the National Endowment for the Arts dance program, and from 1993 to 2000, she was the director of the Pew Charitable Trusts' grant program, the National Initiative to Preserve America's Dance (NIPAD). Since 2000, Snyder has been the president and executive director of Dance/USA, a national arts advocacy organization servicing the United States dance community. Snyder has served on grant panels for numerous state arts councils and arts foundations. She is an officer of the board for the American Arts Alliance and a member of the 2005 inaugural *Dance Magazine* board of advisors. In 2001, she received the Congress on Research in Dance Award for outstanding service to dance research. Snyder holds a bachelor of science degree from American University and a master's degree in arts management from New York University. She has been a dancer and technique teacher, and an adjunct professor in arts administration at American University.

SETTING THE SCENE

Andrea and I shared a sunny afternoon in a New York University dance studio, where the memories of her own journey flowed out with honesty and humor. A dancer to her very marrow, Andrea related the choices that led her to become a crucial advocate for dance on a national level. Hers is a story that is an inspiration to any dancer, especially those feeling anything less than completely successful if they find themselves gravitating toward a dance career "behind the scenes."

— R.C.

Q: How do you describe what you do to other people?

AS: Well, I am an arts administrator with a particular focus and passion for dance. In that capacity, I've dealt with all of the nonartistic sides of managing and keeping an organization intact: company management, where I have been responsible for taking a company on the road, touring, and booking; fund-raising; personnel and human resource issues; and financial management, trying to figure out how to keep a company afloat. I would consider that these jobs are just as creative as choreographing; only you're creatively using a different side of your brain. You're creative in crisis-managed structures because you're often not able to think in advance or sit back and plan. Even if you try to do that, nine times out of ten someone comes walking in the door, or on the telephone, and completely derails the path that you were taking or the plan that you had for the day and you have to shift and juggle in order to deal with the crisis. You keep going to accomplish the things that you need to do.

So, I consider my job in arts administration, or in dance administration, as equivalent to what I would have been had I been a dancer. Which I suppose has kept me going in the field because otherwise, why would I do this? The fortunate part about it is that I've had such incredible experiences working with very creative people at all levels and in all parts of the field, whether it's literally the artistic side or it's other incredibly passionate, knowledgeable, and intelligent administrators or managers. Or it's been board members who have been really gung-ho to do something for the organization or company they're with. Or it's my peers, and peers not just in dance, but also in other fields and disciplines. I feel lucky that I've been exposed to all of these other kinds of connections that I don't necessarily think I would have been had I just been a dancer. So there's the plus to that.

Q: Do you consider your involvement with dance on this level to be your profession, your career, your work, your passion, your calling? All of the above? None of the above?

AS: I consider it pretty much all of the above. My folks and my family said I danced before I walked. I took lots of different types of dance as a child and then I let it go in high school—peer pressure and all kinds of other things. Except musical theater was definitely always there as an undercurrent.

When I made what I think was my declaration of independence from my parents, I said, "I want to be a dancer, and I'm going to be a dancer." I was in my second year of college at American University not having had any clue when I walked into college what I wanted to do. It was 1969, and it was a particularly fragile time for the country. For kids going into college, it was like you were walking right into marches and the antiwar movement. But in my second year of college, I took an Intro to Modern Dance course with Naima Prevots at American University. Naima was one of these inspirational visionaries of dance. I mean, she was totally passionate and committed, and extraordinarily savvy about how to create a dance environment where there was nothing. There were about ten or twelve of us. That was it. And we were her guinea pigs. When I took this class, I was blown away! This was totally cool. Somewhere in the middle of the fall, one of the students came to me and said, "Listen, one of the dancers in my piece just injured herself. We have a student concert coming up, would you like to replace her?" And I think I just flew over the moon! I had barely taken any modern dance, and someone was asking me to dance in her piece! I said, "Yes. Absolutely!" And I was totally hooked.

So that fall, I said to my parents, "I'm going to be a dancer." And therein lay the problem. Because I didn't have any clue or any appreciation for what that meant. And all the questions that parents ask, they asked. "How are you going to make a living?" and "Have you researched the job market?" and "We don't want you to be a gypsy," you know, and "Are you sure this is what you want to do?" I had no answers for them. None. All I could say really from my heart was, "This is what I want to do."

So, I started pursuing a dance career in college, and lo and behold, somewhere underneath all of my passion was some pragmatism that my parents had also instilled in me. When I got out of college, after having a very difficult time making my own choreography, I went into teaching. There weren't very many other options. [*laughter*] I think I had my first midlife crisis just as I was graduating college, saying, "What the hell am I doing? I'm twenty-one years old. How do I make a living?" I got a job teaching dance in a private school in Washington and danced with a few people for a couple of years. And in short order, it became apparent to me, going through all kinds of early life experiences that I needed to change something.

So, I made a choice in 1975 to leave Washington and move to New York City. I didn't know what I was thinking; I just had to try it. I came to New York and got a job with the Dance Notation Bureau[1] right away, as Mickey Topaz's assistant. That set me up for understanding the nonartistic, management side of the field, even though I wasn't really a manager. I was still taking classes, and I auditioned immediately and was accepted by Dorothy Vislocky to dance with her. Dorothy had been at the American University Summer Program at Wolf Trap, which I had taken for several summers. I had studied with the likes of Erick Hawkins and Twyla Tharp, and the Graham Company and Don Redlich, and all these greats who were coming through. So I was exposed to some of the best. And also, because of the intensity of the summer program, they knew the dancers coming out of it. I mean, they knew your face and they knew who you were. So when I went to New York, Dorothy knew me, and she said, "Come and dance with me." But, it wasn't a completely successful experience. It might have been my own lack of confidence about really being a dancer, or the fact that the strings were still sort of linked to my parents way down deep, and I didn't have the guts to really go the distance to know if I could have joined a professional dance company. I didn't push myself that far.

Instead, what I started doing was moving toward management, almost naturally. I had good organizational skills. I was tall so I looked like I knew what I was talking about, even when half the time, I didn't. And so, after this experience with Vislocky and being with the Dance Notation Bureau, I was at a loss about what I really wanted to do.

For a period of time, I went to work in the for-profit sector with Champion Papers. I would run out of there to take classes with Alfredo Corvino and Betsy Hague, but there was no purpose in it because I wasn't sure whether I was going to go back and dance or not.

There was one wonderful moment during that time. I was taking classes all along the way with various people, and there was an audition for the road show of the original *Chicago*, just after it was on Broadway. Here was my dream from way back a million years ago, about being a Broadway hoofer. So, I went to this audition. It was an open call, not a union call. There were about 250 different-sized and shaped bodies, some of whom I knew from classes. We all had on our numbers. I had told my boss at Champion Papers that I had a dental appointment, thinking, you know, that I was going to be back in an hour. We warmed up, they gave us a class, and they taught us the patterns. In groups of twenty, you would get up and do your thing, and the numbers were going, and my number was still there! And I was still there! And then other people were leaving, and I was still there! I was running out to make phone calls to my office, saying, "I'm sorry I'm so late, but, you know, the dentist is really taking a long time." And I stayed and they never told me to leave. Finally, I was amongst the last twenty. Now mind you, physically I have all the makings of a Fosse dancer, long, long legs and neck. Right?

So then they said, "Well, you need to sing now." It had been several years since I had studied any singing, and I clearly wasn't going to cut the mustard with that. So I sang and they said, "Thank you, good-bye." I walked out of there saying, in my mind, "If I had wanted to do this badly enough, I would have been there". It would have been among the things that I could have chosen to do. I know now that I could have always been a Broadway dancer. I also know now that being a Broadway dancer would have meant doing the same thing day in and day out, eight shows a week. After being exposed to modern dance and new choreography all the time, it wasn't as appealing. I left it and never went back to another audition, never needed to go park myself in a jazz class again, or think that I needed to go to study music and singing.

So, I went back to thinking about how I was going to make a commitment to dance and be part of it, but not necessarily be a performer. Because I had the drive to be in dance, but I didn't necessarily have that ultimate, incredibly maniacal passion to be a performer. Within that same year, I applied for and got a position as associate administrator at the Cunningham Dance Foundation.[2] This was in '78–79. My responsibilities included domestic bookings and annual solicitations. I basically learned on the job. One of the things I did at Merce's was to serve as the Cunningham Company liaison to Kirk/Singer Productions, the producers who were presenting Cunningham Events[3] at the Roundabout Theatre. I'd speak to them on behalf of management, setting up the gala event, and ticketing and all the things that had to be done. And immediately after that, they turned around and said to me, "We'd like you to become our executive assistant." Well, here I had been at Merce's for nine months, not quite a year. These people were very intriguing. They were involved with producing a benefit for the New York City Ballet at the Waldorf-Astoria. They told me that as their executive assistant, I was going to be their top dog. And as they grew, I was going to be on the front of the line. In my naiveté, or maybe my stupidity, I decided to leave Merce and go to work for Kirk/Singer Productions. That was in '79. In the course of that year, we produced seven benefits for the likes of the New York City Ballet and Dance Theatre of Harlem, a benefit for what became the New York School of Skating connected to John Curry, a tour of the Soloists of the Royal Danish Ballet, and John Curry's Ice Dancing at the Felt Forum and then at the Minskoff Theatre. I was their only staff. There was nobody else. I taught dance for the skaters who were part of the New York School of Skating. [*laughter*] My paychecks bounced, oh, maybe once every two months. And at the end of that, well, sort of the middle of that year, I realized that I had made a mistake—that my decision to leave Merce had been a wrong decision.

But ultimately, even the wrong decision became the right decision, because I turned around and decided I needed to go back to graduate school. I applied to NYU Tisch School of the Arts and was accepted as a full-time graduate student after seven years of being on my own. I was going to get an MFA in dance at Tisch because I still had this craving to be a dancer. I hadn't given it all up. I was pretty good, except I didn't know if I was really good. I was okay-good. During my first year there, part of the eye-opening process was that I realized that the graduate program at NYU at the time was really not much more than a glorified undergraduate program. I had gone through an undergraduate program, and I had studied dance with all kinds of wonderful people, and I was side-by-side with people who really had no training whatsoever. We were basically taking undergraduate level courses with a few other courses thrown in.

Within that first year, I applied to be a graduate assistant but I didn't get the position. It became apparent that I couldn't continue to be a full-time graduate student without having some kind of support system underneath me. I said to the program, "I'm really sorry, not getting the graduate assistantship means I can't stay here." They turned around and said, "Well, our administrator's leaving, would you become the administrator of the Dance Department? You can get the rest of your master's covered by the school." I moved out of the program, started taking administration classes through the Gallatin Division,[4] and was administrator for the dance program at Tisch on Second Avenue, first under the leadership of Stuart Hodes and then Larry Rhodes.

I basically made up my own master's degree. For my thesis, I decided to produce the first alumni concert for the dance program at the School of the Arts and create a scholarship fund for the school. I produced the whole thing, lock, stock, and barrel, soup to nuts on the fifth floor of Tisch. Just after that was over, and while I was waiting to graduate and get my thesis approved, I was supervising a concert at the School of the Arts on Second Avenue and was introduced to John Killacky, who at the time was Laura Dean's manager but was leaving the position. He said I would be great for Laura. So, right after graduation, I went to work for Laura Dean as her executive director, company manager, fund-raiser, and board liaison. There was no other staff except a TD [technical director] on call when they were touring. We had a couple of gigs ADF [American Dance Festival]; Tokyo; and a tour of Lincoln, Nebraska, and five cities in California, but Laura was beginning to float into her own transition as well. At the end of the second year, she fired everybody, me included, and closed down shop. That was in 1985...I was there '83 to '85.

For the first time in my life, I was on unemployment, thinking that I would hate it. I actually loved it. [*laughter*] It gave me the freedom to go and take classes again and talk with people. And in the course of that period of time, I had lots of conversations with a lot of different people. I went back to people in Washington, and one woman I talked with, Ann Murphy, who at that time was the head of the American Arts Alliance, said to me, "You know, it sounds to me like you've been pretty much a self-starter, and you've actually taken on these tremendous responsibilities without having a lot of time or ability to make mistakes. Maybe it would be good if you were to actually find a job where somebody else was your boss." I came back and really thought that through.

Q: Were you still dancing?

AS: Not much by then. I had sort of moved into administration. The last time I had performed was 1981. And after a few months of freedom, I went to work for Sheldon Soffer Management in the winter of '85. Sheldon was sort of an icon in the booking and dance world. I mean, he had a tremendous roster of dance artists, special acts, and classical musicians and orchestras. My specialty was dance and my area of the country was the Southeast and Mid-Atlantic. I had to book everything for that region, classical musicians as well as dance companies. I learned a lot from that experience. I could do my work and I could go to dance at night, and, you know, I had a life. I mean, you never really had a life when you were doing this 24/7. And I was not really dancing much by then. I went to classes and thought, "What am I doing this for?" It wasn't satisfying, because there was no purpose in it anymore. I had pretty much stopped. I was doing a little Pilates.

Then, near the end of 1986, I actually had a gallstone problem and had to have my gallbladder removed. Just about that time, things in New York were sort of looking pretty grim for me. I hit a slump, and I was not happy in my personal or professional life, and it was like, "Wait a minute, what's going on here?" I needed a change. And my body was telling me it needed a change.

Meanwhile, a friend of mine who was in Washington told me that the assistant director's position in the dance program at the NEA [National Endowment for the Arts] was open, and Sali Ann Kriegsman was interviewing. At the Arts Presenters Conference that year, I walked right up to her and said, "I'd like to talk with you. I'm interested in this job." This was the first time ever that I actively thought, "This is a job that I want, and I will pursue it." With my other jobs, I was just lucky; I happened to be at the right place at the right time. So, we went to lunch and talked about the dance field, the NEA, and the job. I told her that I was going in for gallbladder surgery. She said, "Call me when you're back and let's talk." I put my required SF 171 application into the NEA and went in for surgery. About three or four weeks later, I was slowly recovering. I called her and said, "I'm still interested, and can we talk?" So, I went down to Washington for a couple of interviews and was offered the job, and three weeks later, I started working at the NEA. This was in April of '87.

Working at the Endowment was truly an extraordinary experience. Not only was I learning about all forms of dance from all over the country, but I was learning about all disciplines. I had amazing, keen friendships with people who were incredibly passionate and intelligent about their art form. Then the culture wars started with Serrano and Mapplethorpe,[5] and the whole world imploded for us. We spent the next five years, pretty much, fighting that battle. But also trying to do good things for the dance field. I loved it and I hated it. It was an amazing, amazing life. We worked 24/7 for six and a half years of hard labor. You didn't have any time to do anything else. I learned a tremendous amount, I made great friends, and I got to know the field. I was opened up to a whole different part of the dance field that I had not been exposed to in New York.

Q: Was it bigger than you thought it was?

AS: Oh, it was much, much bigger…

Q: What was your actual role?

AS: As assistant director, I was involved a lot with creating panels, constructing responses for congressional justifications, following up on grant activity through the specialists in each of the departments, making sure that the rest of the program was running, discussing strategic planning with Sali Ann. We spent a lot of time and a lot of late nights talking about where, what, and how. How do we get more money for the dance program? How do we support the underbelly of the dance field and still find money for new things? It was really intense and exhausting. At the end of that period of time, or just about toward the end of that time, I kind of thought, "You know, I need a break from this." We felt beaten up all the time, you know? We had a clipping service and every day there would be an inch-and-a-half-thick pile, filled with opinions and editorials that were just slamming the NEA without even seeing the work! That was just debilitating, because we knew we were doing such good work on behalf of the country and on behalf of the arts and our field, and we were just getting panned for it.

Again, I had a lucky break. I happened to be at the right place at the right time when the Pew Charitable Trusts was thinking about creating a dance initiative. Cora Mirikitani was looking for a program director to run this thing, which they hadn't quite figured out yet, but they had had some preliminary conversations and think tanks, and so they asked me if I wanted to do it. I was ready to leave the Endowment. Simultaneously, in the summer of 1993, I left the Arts Endowment, I took the new job with Pew, which was housed at the Kennedy Center, I got married, and I moved...all within a matter of about two or three months.

Q: Wow!

AS: It was very exciting, but pretty intense. I designed a program for dance documentation and preservation, calling it the National Initiative to Preserve America's Dance, aka NIPAD. I knew I had funding for the first three years and was told that there would be an evaluation process after that. Out of that process, they determined it should be re-funded and extended for another four years, with another three-year cycle of funding. So by about '99–2000, it was clear that it was probably going to "sunset" after eight years and not get funded for another cycle. In the winter of 2000, the directorship at Dance/USA became available and it made a lot of sense for me to consider taking the job. Having been at the Endowment, and having been an individual member of Dance/USA for many years, I knew the organization, and Bonnie Brooks, one of my predecessors at Dance/USA, had for several years asked me to program their biennial Roundtable. So, I kind of knew a lot about it. I applied, interviewed, and got the job.

Andrea as a young dancer (third from left) at JOL-ART Studios, Inc., North Bellmore, NY

Since then, I think I've had a good run so far at Dance/USA. Dance/USA's role is really both as a leader and as a service provider, or you might call it a *leading service organization* or a leadership and service organization. Whatever you call it, it is there to support and strengthen the dance field and the art form, both within its membership and beyond for the general public and for those who are not members.

Q: What type of things does Dance/USA do?

AS: Well, among many of the things we do is to organize professional development and peer networking. We created Dance/USA on Tour, which is a series of seminars that are customized for the needs of individual communities. These are one-shot half-day or full-day courses—not enough, but it's a start. What we found is that by bringing people together and having a reception and having two days of serious talking, they take the lead.

We also started the National College Choreography Initiative [NCCI] in partnership with the Arts Endowment, which is designed to connect the preprofessional community with the professional community by bringing artists into universities and exposing students to practicing, working artists and their companies. It's not that they don't get high-level training in their schools. This is simply a different exposure.

Let's see, what other things have we done? Well, I think one of Dance/USA's great responsibilities is to provide communication to the field. I write a quarterly member letter to the field. I also send that out to funders because I think it's incumbent upon Dance/USA to keep funders informed about the issues that are happening in the field. I've made a concerted effort to keep information flowing to funders even if it's not necessarily about getting money. Dance/NYC is yet another outgrowth, which is our first branch of a local community-affiliated program.

Those are some of the things that we've been doing. We work on a fairly shoestring budget. We don't have a huge staff. We're only five in Washington now, augmented by several subcontracted staff that deal with particular responsibilities, our field office in New York, our director of research in Saint Paul, and a project manager in California who's running a program for choreographers for the Irvine Foundation through Dance/USA.

Q: Is it as it was at the NEA for you? Is it NIPAD? Is it a 24/7 lifestyle?

AS: Well, NIPAD was…

Q: Like a vacation?

AS: Right, which allowed me to focus some attention on my new marriage and family, and was sandwiched between the NEA, which was 24/7, and Dance/USA, which is 24/7.

Q: Right, and you're back to being the self-starter because you're in charge of it all.

AS: Yup. That's where I'm at! That's my life.

Q: Wow! [*pause*] Well, I think some of these next questions you've answered or touched upon already. But fill in what you still think you might want to say about these. How did you first get introduced to dance? Who were some of the major influences and inspirations in your life?

AS: I think my parents saw that I was a great mover physically. So I guess the whole thing started there. There is a picture of me at age seven, dancing under a huge square scarf, four little girls holding each of its ends. I'm convinced now that we were being taught Doris Humphrey's *Soaring*. That was probably my first exposure to dance. We lived on Long Island, and my parents *loved* the theater and *loved* the arts. My father was into classical music. We would go to see *a lot* of musical theater. I was seven or eight at the time. And then I was at a camp, Camp Watitoh, in Becket, Massachusetts, in 1960. I was eight and a half years old. It was an eight-week sleepaway camp for boys and girls. And there was a dance teacher there, whose name was Gladys Filmus. She taught modern dance classes, and she took us to Jacob's Pillow. So, in 1960, I went to Jacob's Pillow! I didn't know *what* I was seeing. But in some way underneath there, I was already hooked. I *loved* those classes and *loved* taking dance. I went to that camp for six years, and every year, I went to Jacob's Pillow. And then, as I was becoming a teenager, I let all that go. It was not the thing to do.

College was my next pleasure. And that was where Naima was a great influence. I saw Graham for the first time in '69 or '70, at Lisner Auditorium. That was really a mindblower. And I think from there, the next major exposure I had was with Manuel Alum, who had come to teach for an AU [American University] summer program with Paul Sanasardo and came back to set a piece on us at AU. I never worked so hard, but I loved it. We were continuously getting the influences of these great artists, and every single one of them sort of left a little mark on me. Hawkins and Limón...I mean, we were exposed to it all. I was getting this HUGE, wonderful modern dance experience. It was just great.

The next influence I would say was a board member at Laura Dean. Her name was Elaine Malsin. She was wonderful, very helpful, very thoughtful, and very wise. I really took to heart a lot that she said.

Q: And in the administrative realm, any influences?

AS: Well, Martha Lohmeyer and Art Becofsky at the Cunningham Dance Foundation. They were models for me at the time. They taught me what I was dealing with...you know, I think back now... the people that I've had the opportunity to work with have been such incredible resources and such brilliant thinkers about work and about the art form. Larry Rhodes was one of the most patient, thoughtful, focused, visionary educators (not to mention having been a brilliant performer). Of course, Sali Ann really has such an amazing wealth of knowledge and thoughtfulness, care, and passion for the art form that I couldn't help but hope some of it rubbed off on me. It was just wonderful to be around her!

[*pause*]

Q: And some of the challenges that you faced along your journey? What are some of the choices you've had to make? Were there some difficult choices, or choices that stand out as exceptionally good ones? Are the choices in retrospect you might have made differently? You mentioned that you just fell in to many of them.

AS: Well, yeah, the bad choices…choice is always good and change is always good, and that's one of the things I've learned. Even bad change is good change, because it gets you off of where you are. So I had to learn that at some point, making the decision to make a change is a good thing, and even if it's a bad choice, it'll get you toward the right path. The other thing I learned in that period of time when I was out of work is that there's absolutely no security in this world. None. And truly understanding that there's no security, gives you security. It's a bizarre kind of thing, but as long as you know that there's no security, you don't hold on to it. Therefore, you are able to move. So those are two big lessons that I learned somewhere along the way. I think I learned that I can trust that I'll always be able to find a job, that I will be able to work, and that I will be able to put my energy and my passion to use somehow. And I shouldn't fear that. There was a huge fear in me somewhere, which is probably why I stepped away from being a performer. It was that fear of not having a job and not being good enough. At some point, letting go of that fear was really imperative for me to be able to move on and enjoy what I was doing, and find a lot of satisfaction in the *non*artistic side of being in the dance field.

Q: Do you think there is a reverse pressure for some dancers? That if you aren't a dancer, then you're copping out or *failing*?

AS: For some, yes. But my admiration for people who are in administration and for what they have to go through equals my incredible admiration for people who painfully put themselves at their own risk to dance. I think there's equality there, and there is a beauty to that when they're *both* appreciated and respected. So, I have all of the respect in the world for people who make a choice to be in the dance field, no matter where it is, whether it's administration or teaching or writing or whatever. I mean, you're doing it because you love it and you find something so fully satisfying and nourishing. I think that's far more important for our hearts and our minds than being in a world other than dance. It just doesn't work for me. I tried it and didn't like it. I had said to my folks that I wanted to make a contribution to the dance field. But I didn't know what that meant at the time. And I think I am and I'm happy with what I've been doing. You know, I would love to do more, love to be even more creative, serve the field better. That's what I've chosen to do. And I'm living my life doing it. So I guess I'm really happy with that.

[*pause*]

Q: What are some of the major ideas you would like to relate to dancers struggling to survive and advance in the field?

AS: Hmm…well, you know, it's very clichéd stuff, but…you have to follow your passion. You've got to go the distance, find out, try. If you don't try, you'll never know. And you can always change course, but you've got to try and at least test yourself to see if that's what it really is that makes you alive. Don't be afraid of trying. And you'll know in your heart. Listen to your heart, listen to your guts, and you'll know. If it's right for you, you're on your way. If it's not right for you, you can change it. But if you don't try, you're never gonna know. Whether it's being a performer, teacher, educator, manager, producer, creating something *entirely* new, going out of the box. If you don't try it, but simply think about it a lot, you're never gonna know. And you'll always be wondering if that's what you could have done.

Q: And do you see any significant trends in any aspect of the dance field, either in training or in the attitude of people both in and out of the field, in the subject matter that people are addressing, either artistically or in administration?

[*pause*]

AS: Hah…well, that's a tougher one. Where do I see trends? I think that there is a great concern about the next generation of both artists and managers. Where are they coming from? How will they be able to survive in the field? How can they find the support to bolster them while they're taking on much more than anyone would expect them to? How, in an environment that places a lot of value on lifestyles and high living, does one make that sacrifice to not necessarily have that kind of compensation, and put oneself at the mercy of an artistic director or an artist to support that effort? What are, and how do you find, the resources to keep you going? I think people are really struggling with that. At least the younger generations are—and those who have been in it for some time.

Q: They're used to it!

AS: We're used to it, and we're not there anymore. You know, we're in a different place in our lives, we have different relationships. But for younger generations coming along, the world is not the same as it was. It's not as open and there *aren't* as many resources as there were. This is a particularly difficult time for finding resources to support the art form.

Q: You think it is? I mean definitely when compared to the seventies. But even when compared to the nineties?

AS: Yes. And because of that, artists are not going in the direction that we are accustomed to thinking of artists going into. I don't think in the next ten years we're going to see companies, in the typical way we know companies to be, because they're not going to be able to be supported in the same way. Artists are choosing to work day jobs and make their work in a different way. They're collaborating in groups and finding shared services, but not creating 501c3's. A 501c3, the nonprofit organizational model, isn't necessarily one that works for young artists these days anymore. And does it need to be rethought? We're all talking about it. It's even the conversation that's happening within the funding community. So I think that there are issues about what the future of the art form, its structure, what it will look like. How will artists make work? And how will their support systems be designed to help them make the work? It's an unknown. But the trend now, if there is a trend, is a level of concern about making sure that they, the artists, and their support systems survive.

Q: And from your perspective on the federal level, is that being addressed?

[*pause*]

AS: It's hard to tell at the federal level. I mean, I think the Endowment (there are other federal support systems, but the Endowment is the one that we know most), has weathered quite a significant storm. It seems that it'll *always* be a ping-pong ball for Congress. It'll always be vulnerable. I doubt in the near future whether support for individual artists will be reinstated. Which is really at the beginning of funding. John Munger, the director of research for Dance/USA, once described his understanding of it to me. He described a support ladder in the dance field, where you started as an artist making work locally. You got your friends and people to support you, and then maybe you got support from a local arts agency. As you move along, your state arts agency may have given you support if there was individual support from them, and then you used to go for a Choreographers' Fellowship and you'd get a grant from the NEA. Wow! That was the imprimatur that stamped you as nationally recognized; you were making high-quality work. You got a sizeable grant of five thousand, seven thousand, ten thousand, or fifteen thousand dollars to make more work. And you honed your craft around that. For a couple of years you continued to get fellowships, or then you would start to build your administrative structure around you, then entered into the 501c3 realm, and a company. And you kept moving up that ladder until you hit the big time and you were a dance company getting a sizeable chunk of change. Well, once the Endowment took the Choreographers' Fellowship rung off the ladder, those who were coming in as individuals were competing for the same pot of money as those who were in the middle of the pack trying to hold on. And therein lay the big problem for the midsize, midlevel company. It had no place to go. It couldn't go up, because it couldn't get the resources around them to do that, and it was competing for the same dollars as those who were at the lower rung. And we haven't seen the kind of generational continuity of more people coming in at the lower level and moving up the rungs of the ladder.

Q: When did that happen?

AS: They did away with Choreographers' Fellowships in '94–'95. There's been some real significant change for the field because of that. I think that it's harder to tour. There's less touring than there used to be. There's always the reality that dance is just not a moneymaker. It's a money loser, and so presenters, who are in tight times, are less interested and less able to present dance. So they fall back on what they know, which is more mainstream, less risky work, and that's what we're seeing now.

But I do think that, again, I don't know if it's a cliché or just that we're so used to knowing it, that dance artists and their managers are some of the most creative people in the arts. They will always find ways to keep doing what they do. They just will. And we'll keep helping them.

Q: If you had to pick a reason why you are *still* in this field, what would it be? What is it about this life that you're doing that you love?

AS: I think it's ultimately the interaction with such creative minds, both artistically and nonartistically. These are people who are human at the very core. They care about their work and the body and the human spirit, and that, to me, is much more powerful than anything else. I find that probably the most interesting thing for me is I'm around people who are passionate, lovers of how the body works, and how it can be *expressive* in a million, million, million, million ways.

Q: Do you have a wish for dance for the future?

AS: [*amused chuckle*] Yes, I have this great dream…as I've been in dance, I view it graphically, and I see that I've been on this circle, moving around the circle, whether it's running, walking, skipping, hopping, whatever you want to call it. I've stopped off and I've been a teacher, and I've stopped off and I've been a manager in a company, and I've stopped off and I've been a funder. And now I am running a dance service organization. The only thing I haven't been is a dance presenter. So, I don't know whether that's in the cards for me in the future or not, but that's one area I have not been in. The idea of being involved at the local level at some point, with a community where I am inspiring people to love dance, intrigues me. You know, being the proselytizer, if I have to be the proselytizer. Getting people in there and enjoying it. I just can't understand why people don't enjoy dance.

My other dream is that there's going to be these retirement communities for administrators [*laughter*] where people will come in and bring us their dance work, and we don't have to do anything to make it happen. We can just enjoy it like that. [*laughter*]

But, do I have any dreams for the field? You know, I just have a dream that our culture will revel in the thrill of what dance is. That's very idealistic. Certainly it is *not* realistic. But I dream that dance will step up among the cultural art forms as an equal to opera and theater and music and be *attractive* to people to come to and enjoy and understand and love and do. We will find people more appreciative and more accepting of the tremendous variety of dance that we have in this country and in this world, and enjoy it. And pay for it and *support* it. That's what I hope. Yeah, I think that's it!

Q: Well, thank you, Andrea.

AS: There you go!

NOTES

1. The Dance Notation Bureau (DNB), a registered 501c3 not-for-profit organization, was established in New York City in 1940 to advance the art of dance by creating dance scores using Labanotation, the symbol system for recording movement developed by the Hungarian choreographer and movement theorist Rudolf Laban in 1928. Dance scores function similarly to musical scores, allowing choreographed works to be studied and performed long after the lifetime of the choreographer. Muriel (Mickey) Topaz (1931–2001) was executive director of the DNB from 1978 to 1985.

2. The Cunningham Dance Foundation, a registered 501c3 not-for-profit organization, is the administrative entity that supports the artistic work of choreographer Merce Cunningham.

3. "Event" was the name that Cunningham gave to a form of performance presentation he pioneered beginning in 1964 at the Museum des 20 in Vienna, Austria, in which excerpts from many different pieces of his repertory were performed in one continuous work lasting generally about one or one and one half hours.

4. The Gallatin Division of New York University is a school of individualized study where students create their own curriculum often based on inter-disciplinary interests.

5. Photographer Andres Serrano's "Piss Jesus" (1987), a photograph of Jesus on the cross that he dipped in urine, and a retrospective of photographer Robert Mapplethorpe's homoerotic images that toured seven American cities between 1989 and 1990 ignited a heated debate in Congress in 1989, led by Senator Jesse Helms, questioning the purpose of the National Endowment for the Arts and often referred to in the press as the "culture wars."

Garth Fagan

GARTH FAGAN

"It definitely is a passion. Because you have to be mad, completely out of it, to be in it!"

Garth Fagan was born in Jamaica, West Indies. He began dancing and performing with Ivy Baxter and the Jamaican National Dance Theater. At the age of twenty, he came to the United States to attend college. After an early teaching, performing, and choreographing career in Detroit, in 1970, Fagan started the Bottom of the Bucket, But...Dance Theatre company in Rochester, New York, which is now known simply as Garth Fagan Dance. Fagan has created commissioned works for such well-known companies as the Dance Theatre of Harlem, Alvin Ailey American Dance Theater and New York City Ballet. His collaborations for dance and theater include, among others, the Wynton Marsalis and Don Pullen collaboration *Griot New York* (1991), and *The Lion King*, for which he won a Tony Award, a Drama Desk Award and an Outer Critics Circle Award for best choreography. His catalogue of other awards and honors includes a Fulbright 50th Anniversary Distinguished Fellowship (1996); a Guggenheim Fellowship; a Dance Magazine Award; a Bessie Award; the Monarch Award from the National Council for Culture and Art; the Samuel H. Scripps American Dance Festival Award (2001); and honorary doctorates from numerous universities.

SETTING THE SCENE

I had first seen the Bucket Dance Theatre perform at the Joyce sometime during the mid- to late eighties, long after Garth had more than earned his respected place in the dance world. I remember being a bit awestruck by his forceful dancers and the thematic content that obviously mattered deeply to him. Many years after, I had the chance to see *The Lion King* and was dazzled by Garth's successful integration of modern dance vocabulary within the limits of a Broadway musical format. I left the theater wondering again about Garth Fagan. My trip to Rochester to interview Garth began and ended in a magnificent snowstorm that would have stopped New York City traffic. But, the Rochesterians went about business as usual. The warmth and generosity with which everyone greeted me was anything but snowy and cold, making it feel more like Jamaica than upper, upper New York State.

— R.C.

Q: I'm here with Garth Fagan on a snowy day in Rochester.

GF: An *unusually* snowy day in Rochester. [*laughter*]

Q: So, my first question: how would you describe to someone what you do? Say, to schoolchildren...

GF: Okay...to children I'd say, I come up with the steps for dances, the rhythms of the movement. Well, I don't know how old these children are, so it would depend. But, I'd give them a *rhythm* standing up in place, so that they'd understand *that* big word. And then I'd explain to them what *dynamic* means because the dynamics of the movement are also very important to me. Because you can see certain dances or dance concerts where the dynamic is the same thing from start to finish. That bores me. Some people love it and the world should be varied like that. But for me, I like slow languid, serene moments contrasted with some, well, I couldn't say some "bitch frenetic movements" to children, but I'd say some "mother of a dog frenetic movements"!

So, I'm a choreographer, which means I put steps together. But it also means that I make choices about what I like to see onstage, whether it be a particular movement style, the way the dancers look, the costumes, what have you. For example, I love equality in gender. So much of traditional dance, especially in America, is so ballet-based and so in love with ballet. This does not mean I do not love ballet. In fact, I've choreographed for the New York City Ballet, Dance Theatre of Harlem, Stuttgart Ballet, what have you. So, I love ballet. But in ballet, the women are carried around and supported by the men. They are swans waiting for princes.

The women that are on my stage are contemporary women, who are mommies and can cook and bake, but can also be CEOs of corporations, can drive fast sports cars, ride motorbikes, whatever they want to do. I don't like to see that separation between male and female on my stage. If the men are going to turn fast, then the women are going to turn fast. If the women are going to be subtle and lyrical, the men are going to be subtle and lyrical. So, that's important to me.

GARTH FAGAN

I also believe that there should also be an element of fun in dance—something uplifting and healing in it. Now, of course, there are some pretty dark moments in art, because that's life. But I still don't want doom and gloom for an entire evening. I want something to get people out of the negative things in their life and pick them up.

As a choreographer, I also have to choose the music for the dance. And while dance has its own inherent music in it, it's nice when it is accompanied by music. And for me, dance and music exist on parallel planes, with dance being a preference and music being its complement. So, I have to choose that, too, and it takes a lot of work to find music that I like, and even more important, that the particular *dance* likes and needs. There's some music that I just adore, and I can't do a step to it because it doesn't support dance or it's too sweet or whatever. And I still love the music, it's good music, but it doesn't work for me. So, that's an important part of what I do, too. That's what I do.

Q: Do you consider your involvement and your relationship with dance to be your profession? Is it your career, your work, your passion, your calling; is it all of the above?

GF: It's pretty much all of the above. It definitely is a passion. Because you have to be mad, completely out of it, to be in it! Liz Thompson[1] said having a dance company is a terminal virus. It has to be a very strong passion because it's so crazy.

I used to paint before I decided to have a dance company. And I plan to go back to it in my dotage. But, you know, the canvas and the oil, acrylic, whatever you want to use, doesn't talk back to you! It doesn't get the flu, it doesn't fall in love, it doesn't fall out of love and then the world is over. It doesn't get injured, you know, all those things that humans get. I mean, when my dancers walk in to the studio, I have to do a *quick* psychoanalysis and say, "Oh lord, this is what's happening today. What do I do? Does she need a big hug? Does she need a big screaming at? Does she need both? Does she need to be ignored?" You know, all of that has to go on in order to get the rehearsal to proceed and the dance finished. And all of these things, which in this instance I'm presenting as negatives, are an inherent part of *being*. Things that pilots go through, that nurses go through, that the postal delivery person goes through, okay? But, because dancers are on stage in a lit space and in, to my taste, very revealing, skimpy costumes so you can see the entire body, they're so vulnerable and visible. And if you have a discerning eye, you can spot all of these things and you say, "Oh Garth's not on his game tonight, so and so's not dancing as well as she used to." Yada yada yada, you know, it goes on.

So, I need that passion to give myself enough strength to go back into the fray. To try and come up with the right conclusion, the right healing for this particular dancer. So, to have that strength to support the dancers in addition to all the other things that go on as a choreographer, it has to be a passion.

It's a career, as far as being responsible to the public in presenting well-thought-out and well-rehearsed, innovative ideas. Movement invention is very important to me. I do some movements that some people think are completely *meshuganah*. But to me, it's great movement because it's like something I never saw before. So, I have a lot of that as part of my career. In fact, the people that come back to see my work enjoy and feel this way about movement. And again, I'm so bored with a "this is right and that's wrong" kind of a world. It's not right or wrong, it's just different. And some days I have an appetite for a lovely piece of fish and other days I want rare lamb. And it's still me and they're both doing the same thing in nourishing me. So, I don't have any patience with that. There are some things I prefer to go back and see again and again and again. And there are some things I refuse to ever see again.

The career part of dance for me is also about protecting and developing dancers. Because dancers are just the most maligned, mistreated of all artists. We don't have the strong unions the musicians have. We don't have the unions that actors have. In fact, one of my biggest sources of pride right now is the number of dancers *Lion King* is hiring around the world. Starting with Aubrey Lynch, who was my dance captain in New York and who is now an associate producer of *Lion King*. Nine companies around the world. Now that's some growth for Aubrey as a kid, thirty-six, thirty-seven years old. And then, under him, I have four people teaching and rehearsing in all the productions, and they're making good money, money that I can't pay them in my dance company, or any dance company, even the popular ones like the New York City Ballet. But because musicals play to two thousand people a show, eight shows a week, they can pay them. And these are kids who, when I chose them (and I had one of the largest auditions in Broadway history), were trained as concert dancers. These kids had been to college and had been taking dance all their lives and they understood that dance is more than just showbiz.

Q: Yes, when I see *Lion King*, I don't think of it as a standard musical. It feels more like concert dance choreography.

GF: Right, *Lion King* is not straight musical theater. That's what I wanted and set out to do. I told the producers, "If you want me to do step, kick, turn, jiggle, jiggle, it won't work." And they said, "No, that's why we chose you." I mean, there's nothing wrong with a great *gypsy*[2] ensemble. That has its own *umph* to it, which is great, but what *Lion King* does is open the eyes of the traditional Broadway audience, many of whom have never been to a dance concert, to the wide range of dance that we have in *Lion King*. We have hip-hop, we have African, we have ballet, we have kids fooling around. That was all intended. So, that was another important career move for me.

When the Japanese do *Lion King*, they sing in Japanese, they speak in Japanese, but they *dance* in *Fagan*, and they dance beautifully because it is new and fresh movement to them. And in their culture, you attack everything and you do it to the best you possibly can. It's one of my favorite *Lion King* companies to see. And that tells me that the movement can be translated. I mean, it's still easier for us in America because we have more modern dance, we have more hip-hop. We're a younger country and we're more of a hybrid. But the movement is translatable.

I thought this through when I was doing *Lion King* and I thought, "How can I hire different dancers who are starving and not being able to pay mortgages? How can I educate the public? How can I serve the story of *Lion King*?" And happily for me, some of the music for the dance sequences existed before. But the majority of them were done after my dances, like the "Lioness Chant," which is one of my favorite ones. Lebo and I and Natalie went into a room, closed the door, and she did a movement and he played the piano and I said, a little more here a little less there, da da da, came out of the room and Julie said, "What are you smiling about?" We said, "We've got the dance!" We played it out for her and it was a smash. I mean, with that kind of collaboration, with artists of that caliber—Julie Taymor, the director, Richard Hudson and Don Holder, the lighting designer—everyone was really pumped, everybody was moving forward, and nobody was taking seconds. And that's why it was such a success.

So, *Lion King* was a career move. And while I was doing that, I was still flying from Minneapolis to Garth Fagan Dance gigs. And Norwood Pennewell and Natalie Rogers, my assistants then, were flying back to do shows and whatever. So, that's where the career comes in: You have to guide that. The downside is me. Because I have less time, and I get spread thin, distracted, exhausted, yada yada yada. But life is tough, you do it. Okay. [*pause*] You asked about passion, career, what were the other ones?

Q: Work, profession...

GF: Work, yeah, of course. Profession? Absolutely. Because anything that is not professional, I'm not interested in. Because there's too much hanky-panky when things are not done in a professional manner. Professional means you start on time, you end on time, you get paid this much, you get per diem, you get health insurance. Those are the kinds of things that I work for, to give to my dancers. To keep them on salary. Up here in Rochester, I just can't run out on the street and pick up five dancers to fill in for this concert tonight the way you can in New York, or L.A. or D.C. or in a company with more dancers. In those situations, you can always keep core dancers and bring in filler. But not here in Rochester. So, I had to impress on my board that they had to be salaried. Because they gotta pay that rent and whatever. The world always forgets the dancers. We love what we do. Therefore there's this feeling that we should do it for free. That's perfect nonsense. You can love what you do, but you still have to buy gasoline and Pampers and all the things that regular folks who don't like what they do, have to do. You know, at this stage in my life, I'm blessed that I'm doing something that I love. And I made that choice against my father's wishes. My father was an Oxford man, a doctor in education, and all of that stuff. And he wanted me to be Dr. Somebody. Well, he's now dead and gone and I smile to him every day and I say, "Well, Daddy, I've got nine doctorates. Don't tell me I didn't work for them. I busted my *everything* for them. So, I'm Doctor, Doctor, Doctor, Doctor, Doctor Fagan, so are you happy?"

And he was happy. The year before he died, I (at his expense, unbeknownst to him, because I used his charge card) flew sixteen dancers down to Jamaica to perform down there. This was in '73, when we weren't making any kind of money. But *dumbo* here thought that those dancers would still be with me, and I wanted them to experience Jamaican culture, and to show them upper-class Jamaican culture, people living without the ghetto stereotype. I also took them to the poor sections so that they could see how that was, too.

Well, I told them that my dad wasn't going to come to the show because he didn't like me doing dance. He wanted me to do something more professional. But I told my father, "Dad, I'm staying at the Hilton with the dancers. I have a box reserved for you, and blah, blah, blah." And then, lo and behold, he came with something like an entourage of seven people and filled the box. After the show, he came backstage all sweetness and light, saying, "My son, the choreographer." And everyone's looking at me and saying, "This was the monster you talked about?" [*laughter*]

And after all that, he flew me back down in about two weeks time and said if I had explained to him that my dancing had intellectual substance (that was always important to him; he analyzed everything), and that it wasn't just people running around the stage and throwing up their legs, he would have never fought me in art. I'm so glad we had that chance to talk, because the next year he had a stroke and died and I would have always been plagued by "What would Dad say?" Because that was so important to me.

Mom was always there. She loved her damn son, she loved her arts, she never was a problem. And she lived longer to see, enjoy, and run around with all my reviews and tell every perfect stranger who she was and that her son was just a wunderkind.

[*as if speaking to his mother*] "Oh, Mom, get away."

[*imitating his mother*] "You never know who might want to see this."

[as if responding to his mother] "Okay."

So, I did have that duality in parenting.

So, yes, my dance has to be professional. I got that from my father. He was a die-hard professional and hard-nosed intellectual. And lots of what I hated about him—hate's too strong a word—but disliked about him, especially as a teenager, guess what? I'm just like that. He actually reminded me that my younger brothers and sisters, as I grew up, would say, "You're just like Dad," and I said, "No! I'm a much hipper guy than he ever was." But anyway, that professionalism is very, very important.

And the hard work comes with anything you like to do. If you love gardening, it's hard work—that is if it's going to be good or special. If it's going to be mediocre, well, then you can just *schlep* around. But if it's going to be a good thing, hard work comes. I'm not impressed by anything less.

Q: And a calling? Did you ever feel...

GF: Drawn to it? No, at the beginning it wasn't a calling. I started this company in 1970. It was right after the sixties and all the racial pride for people of color in America that came out of that. And I came to Rochester, to SUNY-Brockport [State University of New York at Brockport] for a summer program, and they paid me very well. And it went like gangbusters. I mean, I was demonic, demanding, and very hip. I had a 'fro to the heavens, you know. Used hairspray and everything to keep it up there, but it was still the thing. And I had a big success with the students in the two graduate courses I was teaching. I was teaching graduate students how to teach "challenged" or "disadvantaged" or some other horrible name they gave students who didn't have all of the typical background of "regular" dancers. They had some name for them; it'll come to me later. But anyway, so I had the grad students who would watch me teach and then I'd talk to them. And then I had the kids who were freshmen in college, without any dance training. And then we put on a show at the end of the year and the show was a big success.

Courtesy of Garth Fagan

Garth and Norma Thompson dancing in the Ivy Baxter Dance Company, 1960

So we took it around the malls to tour with it. Well, at the end of that year, they made me an offer I couldn't refuse. So, I said, "Oh, I'll just stay here for two years, whatever." And then, I suddenly fell in love with all of these kids: Steve Humphrey, who you saw taking class this morning, who's going to be fifty-two April 13th, he was one of the original ones who started with me and met my father and everything. And Priscilla Scott and Mary Greely and Peggy Hewitt. Just amazing people.

And that's where the calling came. I felt if I went on to New York City to teach at a more prestigious school and make more money, I was going to leave these people here and all of this talent was going to go to waste. And then my mother, of course, being the saint that she was, said, "Of course, you have to just stay there and take care of them," because that was how Mom saw the world. My dad would have said, "Go to New York City. That school is more prestigious. You'll get more money. Go there." Anyway, things happen for a reason. And I kept putting it off and putting it off and putting it off.

And then the company became a real, viable tool for me. In '74, we performed at Jacob's Pillow, on a show with the New York City Ballet, Ritha Devi, and us. At that time, the Pillow used to mix their programs like that. I mean, we were dancing with New York City Ballet dancers like Helgi Tomasson and Gelsey Kirkland and everybody like that. But we took the program. Anna Kisselgoff wrote that I was "brilliant" and that "people were going to hear more from this company" and blah, blah, blah. And I said, "Damn, this is the *New York Times*!" So, it was such a vote of confidence for me. We had a dance then called *We Are Somebody* and one called *Roots*, yeah, those are the two that we did, I think. And I was still dancing back then, too. Anna said something like, "All dances we'd love to see again and see more…," something like that. But anyway, to me it said, "Oh, you can do this."

So, I gave myself ten years to try. And when ten years came, the company still wasn't where I thought it should have been financially, because I had a much different understanding of how it worked than it actually did. But the people and the analytical and creative aspect of choreography spoke to me. And it was clearly something that I needed. So, I stuck it out.

Q: How did you first get introduced to dance? What are some of the landmark events in your dance life and who were some of the major influences in your dance life?

GF: Okay, I first got introduced to dance on a fluke. In my high school in Jamaica, Ivy Baxter was one of the first and earliest Caribbean voices in dance, using Caribbean movement in conjunction with modern dance. She had studied in Germany with Sigurd Leeder, and she was teaching gymnastics at my high school. Well, they had a Christmas production and some guy who was doing a dance sprained or broke his ankle, I can't remember which. And everybody said, "Oh, Garth, you could fill in for him. You could do it!" Because at the time I was a big party dancer. I was winning cha-cha contests and mambo contests and all of that stuff. So, everybody knew me as a party dancer, but modern dance, what's that?

So, anyway, I did the gig, I did the Christmas thing mostly because it would annoy my father, which was important, you know, being a teenager and all. So, I did what she asked me to do and, unbeknownst to me, everyone was impressed. I wasn't impressed 'cause I was so busy trying to keep up and remembering what came next, and who came in where, and when I lifted this one and when I lifted that one, you know. Anyway, afterward she invited me to come to her studio and take classes. Her dance company, the Ivy Baxter Dance Company, ultimately became the Jamaican National Dance Theater after Jamaica became independent in 1962. So, I took classes there and it meant that I got to go on trips out of the Caribbean Islands, to South America and all of that. And there were these lovely parties, so *of course* I'm going to do this. For all the wrong reasons. [*laughter*]

Q: It's not a bad reason. Really.

GF: Right, but nothing philosophically deep, you know. I did it for the trips and the parties and all of that. And wherever we went, we met the heads of state, Michael Manley, Selma Manley. Michael was the prime minister of Jamaica and what have you. So, it was fun! And that's how I got into it.

And then, when I came to America, I studied with Pat Welling at Wayne State University in Detroit. In fact, she co-choreographed my first solo. A piece called *Contemplation*. And it was a big hit. I did it in perfect silence, if you please. It was a big ego trip now that I look back at it, but so what. The critics loved it and what have you. But Pat taught me a lot about just basic choreography. And a lot about, "Well, why not do it? If that's what you want to do, do it. You're sure you want to do another one of those leaps? You just did five. Aren't you tired? You know, but six will bring down the house. So, if you want to do six, go ahead." That was her attitude. Wonderful attitude.

And then I started traveling around, going to every dance concert I could, to see what was on stage. And then I met *Graham*. And there was no company like the Martha Graham Company in the sixties to my taste. It was just heaven. Because the dances had meat, had meaning. The men were strong, they weren't wussy little men running around the stage. They were men. So, that calmed me down considerably. That was very important. And, of course, there was Mary Hinkson. She was so beautiful. And there was Yuriko. It wasn't just a company of blond-haired and blue-eyed dancers. I don't even know if she had any blond hairs and blue eyes in the company, 'cause Martha wasn't one. So anyway…and the costumes, and Isamu Noguchi's stage designs, and the music. It was just a perfect evening in the theater to my taste.

Anyway, that company impressed me immensely, and it became a standard of excellence for me. And then the Ailey company was the next one that did that for me. But to add something about Graham. I remember being in class with her. She wanted us to do a simple, unadorned walk. Never showed us *diddly*. And we kept going across the floor and she'd say, "No," and people kept crying 'cause in those days, you would see Martha simply coming across the campus with her umbrella, and you'd start shaking with excitement because, well, it wasn't her, it was us responding to her. And in those days teachers were not as professional as they are now. They would hit you and talk about you, you know. "Why are you here? What's the matter..."

Anyway, Irene Reins and I went across the floor, I guess, for the twelfth time, just the two of us. By then, everybody else had frizzled out. Martha used to do that to people. But I just kept doing it. And finally, I went across by myself and she said [*clap, clap, clap*], "You're going to go places." And I said, "Yea!"

What I think she was talking about was my tenacity, the fact that I wouldn't give up. I didn't know what the hell she wanted at the time, but it makes sense to me now. What she wanted me to do was to strip from all the shaped arms and all the dancer's walk and all of that crap that we used to do at that time. 'Cause that's how you told the world that you were a dancer. I mean, if you dropped a dime, you'd pick it up in fourth position and carry on. But that moment was such an important lesson for me. Because it stripped away and stripped away and stripped away, 'til it became purer and purer. I wish I had a video of that experience…

But anyway, that was a very important moment in my career. Which is one reason why you don't see my dancers doing grand preparations and all of that stuff. I hate that. You know. You go to some ballet concerts and you see these fabulous preparations and they do two poopy little leaps and two pirouettes and what's that about! But the preparation was *so fabulous*, you know? And I thought I was going to get twenty pirouettes at least. So, I kill my dancers if I see them doing too much preparation. I want it fresh and coming from no place, the way lots of the primal peoples danced before there was ballet, before there was Europe. You know, the Asians, the Africans, the people of native America here, they were all just *dancing*. They didn't have classes, they didn't know first through fifth position, none of that crap. The Watusi, in Africa, they do some bitch jumps, and they don't get shin splints. Because they use the legs correctly and because they keep doing it from childhood through adulthood. And here you've got dancers with Marley and sprung floor and they're so fragile. Anyway, that lesson back with Martha in simplicity and basics was important.

Q: What about nondancers in your work?

GF: Steve Humphrey was a wrestler when I got him in the company. I also got a lot of dancers from the soccer field. I was big into soccer. And I was taken by people I saw dancing beautifully at parties, or moving well on the basketball court or the soccer field. Or I'm inspired by the fast movement of those sports car drivers. I was a sports car fanatic. I even used to drive a TR4 at one time.

Q: Okay, in some of the literature you gave me, you mention Pearl Primus and Lavinia Williams as influences also.

Courtesy of Garth Fagan

Fagan at home in Rochester, circa 1972

GF: Yeah...Pearl and Lavinia. Lavinia came to Jamaica to teach classes every year or two. She had more of a ballet background than Ivy Baxter. And a back, oh God! A real supple, fluid back. Lavinia was very important because she taught me a lot about the back. And a lot about presence and stillness. With Ivy, it was everything: rhythm was predominant, and technique was important, and her fluidity was superb. But Lavinia had this thing about the back, the Yanvaloo[3] that she brought with her from Haiti. And her presence was extraordinary. So she was very important for me.

And then Pearl Primus from Trinidad would come in to our Jamaican tribe. We would do an afternoon's rehearsal with her and then we'd perform that evening. You know, it was lots of African-based ritual stuff. You did four of these and eight of those and whatever, so it wasn't all that difficult. But she taught me economy of time and self-confidence. Her husband, Percival Borde, also worked with us in those amazing afternoon rehearsals. So all three of those ladies, in that order, one, two, three, were great influences: Ivy would be number one, Lavinia number two, and Pearl would be number three. I learned a lot from them.

Q: And what are some of the major challenges you have faced along your journey to this point? What are some of the choices you had to make? Were there difficult choices? Are there choices that stand out as exceptionally good ones? Are there choices in retrospect that you might have made differently?

GF: There are everyday choices, like not going to a dinner party and staying home and listening to your music, say, for the five hundredth time, when everybody else is going to the party or whatever. Those kinds of choices were difficult for me in the beginning. Now I love solitude and I work from solitude. That's my hang-up. I'm sure everybody doesn't do it that way, but for me, that's how it works. And there was also the choice of realizing that this wasn't going to make me big money and wondering why I was still doing it. And how, if we were in New York City, we would be further ahead. We'd have richer boards, for instance, that could give us more money than the boards up here. They just don't have the money or the understanding of what it takes to support a company up here compared to a New York City board. And I don't have the Jasper Johnses[4] and all those people around to help me that some people do. You know, all of that stuff. So, that was difficult to understand.

For the first thirty-two years of this company, I taught full-time at SUNY-Brockport. I was spending all my days teaching—technique, choreography—and I became a distinguished university professor. There I was, at the top of the heap, not just at Brockport, but on a statewide level. And then all of my weekends and evenings were about the dance company. That was the way it had to be. So, that was a hard sacrifice. And when I wanted to go party on the weekends or whatever, there was always, "I have rehearsal tomorrow." I was too tired. My back would hurt from having lifted a fat cow in Detroit. Well, that's a side story!

Before I came to Brockport, I was principal choreographer of Dance Theater of Detroit and Detroit Contemporary Dance Company. And there I hurt my back lifting a fat lady. And since then, I have always insisted that the women in my company not be fat because of that reason.

Q: Well, it seems to be in your aesthetic also. I've noticed the tall, very streamlined look you go for. It's a lovely look for your movement.

GF: Yeah, it really works for my movement. I also always have a short one or two ladies. I like the speed. I like the mix. I don't like to see seven maids all in a row. I like to see the tall, the small, whatever. But, because of that back injury, I have always made sure that my men don't have to lift fat cows. [*laughter*] I forgot that part of it. And something else in Detroit that was good for me was that I had a junior high school, all boy, dance ensemble that was fierce and proud and strong and fabulous. They *really* taught me a lot. And then I directed an all-city high school dance company after that.

Those were some important things that I forgot to mention about my formative years. I mean, being in Detroit in the sixties with all of it: Martin Luther King speaking at Cobalt, and the Supremes and the Temptations and all of that, was like heaven. Aretha Franklin, I can't forget that! But, anyway, I don't know how I jumped back to all of that...where were we with your questions?

Q: Choices and major challenges.

GF: Oh, right. The everyday challenge of going back into the studio to work out something that I really did not like. That's one of the most important challenges that any artist can face. I'm very true to that now. If I don't like it, it ain't gettin' out there, you know. I've got to correct it and go back in and work, work, work 'til I get it right. It doesn't mean it's right to everybody or most people, you know. But that it's right to my taste and my eye. That is hard. My family suffers because when I'm choreographing (my grandkids now know "when grandpa choreographing"), in other words, don't f—— with him. Leave him alone. He's not here.

Q: His body's here but he's not in.

GF: Right. They learned that early in the game. I know I could have been more at home for them. But you can't do both things. Martha Graham explained that one to me. I once said to her, "Martha, none of my relationships are working out, blah, blah, blah." And she said, "Well, what makes you think that you're so special?" [*laughter*] That was so important to hear, because, what it is, with people like Martha and me is that the dance is number one, and the partner is number two, and the lover is number three. That's the way it is. And until I came to grips with that (and it took me a long time to figure out even after Martha told me), I didn't understand why I was having so much trouble with my relationships. You give so much of yourself to your dancers in the studio to keep them going and to keep them afloat, that when you come home, you don't want to hear diddly. You know, I just don't want to go there when I come home. Leave me *alone*. I need some space, you know, or some solitude. So, that was a really hard one for me to come to terms with. But, it works. It works. And my grandkids, who are now grown, they've turned out beautifully and I spoil them. I buy them clothes and all that.

But what finally sang home to me was that dance was number one. And that all the other relationships weren't as important to me as the relationship with *The Dance*, that abstract, demanding, bitch of a thing. Now, you know how ungrateful dance is. You don't take class for a week and suddenly nothing works...and you say, "Well, damn it, I can't do this. I don't know what this is about, what happened?"

Q: I know. "It was just one week!"

GF: Yeah, it's just such an ungrateful taskmaster. But, I mean, that took precedence.

And another challenge for me was that what I wanted to see onstage wasn't there. And I had to figure out how I was going to put it there. I wanted to see people of color onstage dancing with a natural pride. By natural pride, I mean, not exalted. Not super-proud. None of that. Just a natural pride that declared, "I'm proud of me, myself, my being, and I'm proud of my culture. And I know that my culture has negatives. But I know that it has more positives than the media puts out there." Ninety percent of the people are really working on their mortgages and their families. The other five or eight percent are doing drugs and living in mayhem, but those are the ones that you hear about again, and again, and again. And I didn't want stereotypes.

I got in deep trouble in the seventies when I had Peggy Hewitt, a blonde, blue-eyed dancer do an African dance I had called *Roots* in an African costume. I got assaulted by both the white people and the black people, from different points of view. But this woman could dance, and she did it beautifully. It is still one of the proud moments in her life. In my mind, this was a technique that anybody could do, which was my whole point. It doesn't mean that you're trying to become a part of the cultural whatever. It just means that you are applying yourself to a technique. The same biases happen when black people and ballet are considered. You know, there is this thought that because we have more butt and longer heels it can't work. Well, yes it can work. It's just a different line, like the line of our beautiful penché *arabesque*, which we do. What did Deborah Jowitt call it? "Faganesque arabesque" or something like that.

Q: They were practicing it in class today.

GF: Yeah, straight arabesque, you know, backs down, not the lyrical one. The lyrical one is fine if you're talking about swans and princes, but I'm not. I'm talking about contemporary people in contemporary lives. I like a clean, pure line. When I did a piece for the New York City Ballet, some of the most fabulous dancers in the world, they actually had a problem with that arabesque because it's surprisingly hard, 'cause you have to give up control of your center.

So anyway, those challenges of having the courage to break traditional lines like that—that interests me. To do jetés with the glutes to the audience as opposed to having the open leg to the audience, 'cause I love the glutes and the roundness there. It's a different line. It's not the purer line of the open leg. But you've got certain globes here [*theatrical gesture of hand to back side*] and that's part of art. Initially people would say, " You can't do jetés like that!" And I said, "Why not? Open your eyes." And we do them the regular way and we do them the reversed way. We do pure chaînés turns, and then we do my rhythmic chaînés turns with the arms changing and the backs contracted. And it's much harder.

But some people don't like changes like that 'cause they know what they studied as little girls and that's the only thing they judge dance by. That's perfect nonsense. If we don't push the art form forward, it's going to go away. Somebody's got to make the changes and make it relate more to current times. So the changes I have tried have been a constant challenge…and then, of course, the tyranny of economics is annoying.

GF: It never goes away. Always *schlepping* for money. You board the plane and you don't get paid until after the gig but you got to come up with the airfare, and the hotel, and the per diem before you even make the money. It's no way to run a business, but it's the only way. And as we have seen the corporate dollars disappear, the foundations tighten to more traditional things. For example, in *Griot New York*, there is a duet where both people are topless. Hah! I mean, there is a large percentage of the world runnin' around without tops. Come on, that's what God gave women to feed our children! What is this playboy attitude about it? Well, that got me in some hot water with certain sections of the public. But when I did the dance, and since it deals with spring and rebirth, I thought, "I'm going to do this." But anyway, that's an example of some of the hard choices that financially can affect me.

My senior dancers, who stay with me forever, help me a lot. Like PJ and Natalie. Sharon just had a baby. Natalie's now pregnant. So, life goes on. That's something you've got to learn, too. That you're going to lose them because of these beautiful, important occurrences in their lives. I mean, those kind of things balance the picture for you.

[*pause*]

Q: What are some of the major ideas that you would want to relate to dancers struggling to survive in the dance world? What would you like to tell them?

GF: Discipline. Discipline. Discipline. It's the reason why *Prelude*, a dance that I open a lot of programs with, has the subtitle *Discipline Is Freedom*. Oy! That was my daddy's thing. Discipline is freedom. Because I was wild as a young man. Of course, I didn't think I was. I thought I was just being my fabulous self and that my daddy was all wrong. But my daddy knew I was a son of a bitch. And if he hadn't held on to me with tight reins and really impressed this on me, "Garth, discipline is freedom," "Garth, discipline is freedom," who knows? And then one day, maybe too many years later, I understood what he was talking about. That's the thing they have to understand. That you've got to take those classes, and you've got to develop the instrument. And you've got to repeat until you get it right, 'til it's unadorned, 'til it's whatever.

And then there's vulnerability. So that when you're in the studio with a choreographer, you're vulnerable. You're open to any and all things. A good choreographer is not going to injure you. We have one or two mad, mad women or men around but you know who

© AP Photo/Kathy Willens

The Lion King, *choreography by Garth Fagan*

they are before you go there. But most of us don't want to injure a dancer. We just want to try and probe for new things. We don't want to do the same things we've been doing. And we don't want to see the dancers doing the same thing in the same way. So, it's about discipline and the vulnerability to work with a choreographer to try new things. Those are on the top of my list for young dancers. And to educate themselves in things other than dance. That you listen to the news every now and then. That you pick up a newspaper and read it. We read reviews of our company and other companies and we discuss them. You know, what was true, what was accurate, what was bias on the writer's part, or the *dummkopf* just didn't get it. You know, yada yada. This prepares them and can protect them for the future because they are thinking on their own.

Q: Do you see a significant trend in any aspect of the dance field? Either in training or in the attitude of people in or out of the field?

GF: Yeah, I think we've gotten so physical. I think lots of what we were bitchin' about—we weren't bitchin', we were just mildly complaining—but, lots of what the old teachers used to do to us, like the lectures, we've lost that. And now we're training these wonderful physical beings. But they might as well be gymnasts or athletes. The passion, the dynamics, the subtlety, the understanding, for example, that this is a Russian piece versus a Cuban piece, they don't get that anymore. And it's making it technical and bland to my taste. I love when the individuality of the dancer comes through the movement. When you know that's so-and-so, and I bet she likes pizza, I bet she doesn't like dogs, she likes cats, whatever. All of those things you might find as direct opposites when you talk to so-and-so. But you're feeling that sort of thing onstage. You're feeling more than just the movement. You're feeling a human being behind the movement. You know? I remember when I had a new girl in the company, and she was always working the audience because that's where she came from. I said, "Darling, we don't do that in Garth Fagan Dance, we bring it all inside. Trust me, the movement will speak, it's big enough, it's clear enough. You just keep a blank face. They'll get the movement." (There are companies, of course, where everybody is really working, wow! It's too much for me.) But, that's what we're *not* teaching them.

Q: And technically, or in subject matter, do you see changes or trends?

GF: It's still the same big technical thing. I love technical things and I love technical dancers. But there seems to be a loss in dynamic qualities. They can do things fast or slow. That middle place, they don't understand. Big or little. Okay. But that in-between place they don't understand. And that beautiful transition, from little to medium to big, or vice versa, they don't understand that. That's something we're losing. And because we've lost so many men as teachers in dance, so many men now are so weak, and so unmale. I've never liked macho idiots. That's not what I'm talking about. That's just phony. But we've lost the testosterone, the maleness of it. I don't care straight or gay. You go to bed with whomever you want to go with. Have a good life, that's all I ask. But there's something called testosterone, which men have, and we're losing that. I mean, Nureyev was as gay as a Chinese funeral, but he was *male*. That's all I ask. So, I don't want us to go back. It's not an antihomosexual thing. It's just a testosterone thing that we're losing. I mean, I want to make that clear. We, as a dance community, are not teaching them that way.

Q: And one last question: What keeps you going? What's still driving you?

GF: That word "passion" comes up again. I have a passion for it. And I need to solve more problems in dance for myself, and hence, for the dancers and the audience and the critics. I also have a passion to really come up with a viable and different technique that involves all of the things that I love in movement, like the speed and precision of ballet without the preparations and the artifice. Because I love creating surprises, so that you don't know what is going to happen next in movement. I just love those surprises. And placement is important and line is important. And the supple back that I talked about earlier. I mean, there's good traditional line and there's my line. And it's clear when the two change. And the dynamic changes I love are in my technique so that my dancers can give you all that dynamic range on the stage. Because I love changes in dynamics. It's my hang-up. Shoot me.

Q: So in your mind, is there still room for your technique to evolve?

GF: Not so much to evolve it as codify it. I think it's very much there now. We've gotten five Bessie Award[5] winners out of it! You see the dancers it has produced. Men and women. And they are fearless. And that's important to me. It's not like, "Whoops, am I going to be able to do this?" No. Let's do it. And if you blow it, you blow it. Let's do something else, and you keep on going. It's not, "Mea culpa, mea culpa, mea maxima culpa." But to kind of codify it would be the next step. It's such a difficult technique, and they do two classes a day. They do the eleven to one class you saw and then they come back at six and they do another class. We don't get injuries because of that, because it includes a real warm-up before you get out there on the stage. You know? It's your goddamn instrument, take care of it, and it'll last longer. I mean, you've got to really warm up. Look at Steve. Fifty-one, fifty-two next week and look at him!

Q: Do you have a dream for dance for the future? For yourself for the future?

GF: I just wish we could get paid more for what we're worth and that people could understand how important American modern dance is to the art fabric of the world. How cutting-edge we are. How diverse we are. How important we are as far as spending an evening with the arts. I mean, we shoot ourselves in the foot a lot, with those dumb articles we write.

Q: With everyone criticizing everyone else?

GF: Yeah.

Q: It's counterproductive.

GF: It's very counterproductive and you can't do that. As opposed to talking about what you do and realizing that your way is not the only way. It is not, and everybody is not going to love your way.

Q: I think it's getting a little bit better than it was, say, in the sixties and seventies. Don't you think?

GF: Yes, I hope so. But I still see some dumb articles. I mean, omissions and quarreling like that, I don't understand. I just don't understand it. Maybe because it's humbled me in my career and I'm not in New York politicking. But it seems to me that we've got to get over the politics of it. That's one thing I wish for in the future…

[pause]

Q: Well, I think this is a great place to stop. I mean, I could go on and on, like the snowstorm. But for now, thank you very much!

GF: Okay. Do you want to go get something to eat?

NOTES

1. Liz Thompson, a choreographer and dance administrator, has served as director of the Lower Manhattan Cultural Council, the vice president of the Next Wave Festival at the Brooklyn Academy of Music, and executive director of the Jacob's Pillow Dance Festival.

2. "Gypsy" is a nickname for Broadway chorus dancers who often spend much of their creative lives performing in touring productions because, like gypsy peoples, they have a romanticized nomadic lifestyle.

3. Yanvaloo, a ritualistic dance of the snake goddess Dambahla in the Haitian vodun pantheon, is based on a wavelike successive movement of the spine.

4. Jasper Johns (b. 1930–) is a painter, sculptor, and printmaker widely celebrated as one of the most influential artists of the post-war era. His work, in which he frequently appropriated well-known images such as targets, flags, maps of the United States, and commercially stenciled numbers and forms as the focus of his explorations into the relationship between media and form, has been credited as the inspiration for many art movements such as pop art, minimalism, and conceptual art. He created the environment or set designs for many of Merce Cunningham's dance works.

5. The Bessie Awards, often referred to as the modern dance Oscars, were named for the dance composition teacher Bessie Schoenberg. They are administered by Dance Theater Workshop and awarded annually at a ceremony in New York City.

Joann Keali'inohomoku

106

JOANN KE

JOANN KEALI'INOHOMOKU

"It's like you've put some little dried thing in a pan of water and it begins to swell. That's what my reaction is like....I'm just so filled with it all."

An early pioneer in the field of dance anthropology, Joann Keali'inohomoku is a true scholar, holding B.S.S. and M.A. degrees from Northwestern University and a Ph.D. in cultural anthropology from Indiana University. Keali'inohomoku's dance training has included work in the ballet and modern dance idioms with such masters as Martha Graham, José Limón, and Jean Erdman, and ongoing studies in Scottish, Spanish, Irish, Japanese, and Korean dance; international folk dance; and many Native American dances for over sixty years. Keali'inohomoku's revolutionary article "An Anthropologist Looks at Ballet as a Form of Ethnic Dance" sent shock waves that are still felt in the dance history, education, and criticism communities since it first appeared in *Impulse* magazine in 1970. She has written and presented papers at conferences in over seventeen states and throughout the world, including South Africa, Mexico, Holland, and Canada. From 1970 to 1996, Keali'inohomoku taught on faculty in the Department of Anthropology at Northern Arizona University. In 1981, she founded Cross-Cultural Dance Resources, Inc. (CCDR) in Flagstaff, Arizona, an organization dedicated to research, consultation, and performance in the area of dance anthropology. In addition to over fifty years of fellowships, grants, and awards for her field research in dance, Keali'inohomoku was the first recipient of the Congress on Research in Dance (CORD) Outstanding Contribution to Dance Research Award (1996) and in 2000 had an award instituted in her honor by the Southwestern Chapter of the Society for Ethnomusicology.

SETTING THE SCENE

When I first read "An Anthropologist Looks at Ballet as a Form of Ethnic Dance" in graduate school, I let out a sigh of relief. It was a refreshing way to look at ballet that explained to me some of the reasons why I both loved and disliked ballet. Time after time, the article would come up in conversation over the next fifteen years until, finally, I met Joann Keali'inohomoku and the door to the world of dance anthropology flew open for me. When I traveled out to meet Joann, there she was in the open air of Flagstaff, surrounded by the countless treasures that envelop her in a sort of "sympathetic magic" as she would say, with dance. Her tireless work for Cross-Cultural Dance Resources and her research is her life. Dances that very few people who attend ballet, modern, and/or any proscenium concert dance will ever see or hear of, live and breathe in her magical world.

— R.C.

Q: How do you describe what you do to people who are not in your field or in the dance field? For example, you are at a cocktail party and someone asks, "What do you do?"

JK: Well, I don't think I've been very successful in telling other people what I do and what I want to do. But one of my goals has been to let people realize that dance is not just twinkle toes and something superficial and so on like this. I've wanted to tell them that it is critical, that it is universal in its voice and power. It's one of the reasons why I always use the word "dance" instead of some alternative word like "movement." In fact, I think the one thing that has astonished a lot of people is just that very statement, that dance is universal. It's found in every human society, and many people will say, "Oh, I never thought of that." Then my next line is, "And if there's something that is universal in every human society, then it must be important to human beings." And the thing that's so unusual about it is that while it's universal to human beings, it's always culturally specific. Each culture has its own idea about who, what, when, where, why, and how the dance occurs. But they all have dances. There is no society that doesn't have dances. I find so often that I have to keep repeating that.

Q: So do they ask you if you are a dancer?

JK: Well, a lot of times they do. [*laughter*] And I say, "Yes." I think one of the things that maybe gives a little credibility to what I say is that I'm an anthropologist. And the reason I think it gives credibility is because if they do have that image, as the *new Westerners* do, that dance is superficial, that it is a twinkle toes activity, when I introduce the idea of being an *anthropologist* who is studying dance, it sounds like maybe it's more substantial than they thought. But a lot of time, I don't get any further feedback. I'm sitting at the cocktail party, and I say what I say, and they say what they say, and I never hear from them again. So I don't have that feeling that I really sent this message out over the whole world. It seems that there is this very narrow idea about what dance means. But every culture has that narrow idea.

Q: Really?

JK: One of the things I found out is that a lot of times people are not interested in somebody else's dance, so the message that it's universal doesn't really matter much. Even in Bali. They think, "We want to do *our* dancing. We feel that *our* dancing is important, but *their* dancing, well, we don't know anything about that."

Q: Do you think we like our dances because it pleases us kinesthetically, or because it is known to us, or what do you think?

JK: Well, that's probably a part of it. But I think it's part of an ethnocentricity where everybody esteems their own values, their own language, their own music, their own dance, their own way of bringing up children, their own whatever it is. This is the thing you're comfortable with and this is the thing you use to measure everything else by. And everything else is a little bit exotic, but that doesn't necessarily mean you're interested. The West tends to be more interested in other cultures than other cultures tend to be interested in the West, except for the fact that ballet and concert dance have attracted other parts of the world.

When I spent time in Hawaii and in different places in the Pacific, I'd sometimes try to talk about some of my work with Native Americans. Well, they just weren't interested! They really didn't care! They're interested in their dance. And the same thing with the Native Americans. I tried to talk to Hopi about what Hawaiian dance is like—they don't care! [*laughs*] I mean they might think it was fun to have a party with a Hawaiian theme so everybody can pretend to do the hula-hula or whatever, but that's about it.

Q: Do you consider your involvement with dance to be your profession, your career, your work, your passion, a calling? All of the above? Maybe something else?

JK: [*soft chuckle*] Well, I don't know how much time you've got. But, okay, I guess you really want to know, because it's all of the above, yes. I'll just start at the very beginning.

I was born in 1930 in Missouri, and as you may know, the whole bottom of the economy fell out in 1929 when my mother was pregnant with me. So here I was with parents who were very well educated and very knowledgeable about the ideas of child rearing and so on like this, and wanted to give me every opportunity but they didn't have any money. I mean they were very badly damaged by the Depression.

My mother was very innovative in figuring out several ways that we as a family could experience wonderful things on a shoestring. I was an only child until I was ten, so when I'm talking about my family, it was just three of us. When I was three years old, we moved to Chicago, where the World's Fair was going on. My mother was a musician, and in Chicago, she taught and played the piano for dancing classes at Navy Pier so I could take dance lessons. Well, as part of the fair, there was this big dance school with its own company. Every weekend they performed *Cinderella*, and I and a little boy got to dance in the ballroom scene. Although I was only three years old when I danced in that, I remember it. And because I was a performer, we were able to come in every weekend and see other events for free. I saw groups from all sorts of countries, Germany, Japan, any country you can think of that was at the fair. And they all had some kind of a booth or performance. And then my mother ushered for groups like José Greco and Azuma Kabuki. So, I was seeing all of these wonderful things!

There were also several places that were free on Sunday after sundown in Chicago. One Sunday we'd go to the Field Museum, one Sunday we'd go to the Art Institute, one Sunday we'd go to the planetarium, one Sunday we'd go to the Museum of Science and Industry, and if it was nice weather we'd go to Jackson Park and the Japanese gardens. So you see, I was seeing the world. I had this tremendous education that didn't cost them anything.

Of all of the places that we went, the place that I loved the most was the Field Museum. I think I must have been a born anthropologist because I loved to see what people were doing and the displays of people fighting or dancing or whatever it was. I loved to see the mummies and all of those different kinds of things.

But, back to the Japanese gardens for a minute. In Jackson Park in the early thirties, there was a beautiful Japanese garden. The Japanese couple who ran the place were attracted to me as a little girl who was interested in everything. Well, they gave me a Japanese doll, and they told me about different kinds of Japanese things. I was *so* interested in Japan. I thought, "Oh, that's my favorite culture in the whole world." And then I had a friend who went to San Francisco, and she brought me back a Chinese opera doll, and I said, "Oh, no, that's my other favorite one!" I was gaga about all of them. So I started collecting dolls and doing my own sort of research about their cultures. You know, about why do they wear this costume, and so on. I was about five years old and, I guess, just a born researcher.

Then, when I was seven years old in 1937, my father told me that the Chinese and the Japanese were at war. And my little seven-year-old heart was just broken to think that my two favorite cultures were at war with each other. So apparently I said, "It's because they don't know about each other's dances. If they knew about each other's dances, they wouldn't be able to fight." [*chuckles*] So at the age of seven I decided I wanted to grow up and I wanted to learn about all the different dance cultures, and somehow be able to write about them or teach them or something like that. I never had the idea that I wanted to learn how to do them, because part of the beauty of it was the people who belonged to that culture were doing it. Not me doing somebody else's culture, but them doing it.

So I became what I am now when I was very small. The dedication, the passion really was articulated at the age of seven. But, I didn't know the name "anthropology." Well, I went off to Northwestern University and started as a school speech student. Other people wanted to be performers, or directors, or teachers, or something like that. They'd say to me, "What do you want to do?" And I'd say, "Uh, experimental theater." I didn't know what else to say. [*giggles*]

Then I took a course in anthropology, because it fulfilled some of my requirements. The professor was Melville Herskovits, who was very interested in music and dance. We used his textbook, and he said we would "move in the field of music, theater, and drama, grossly ignored by scholars on all sides of the anthropological world." I still have that textbook where I wrote to myself in the margins, "That's it! That's what I'll do."

I was nineteen, and I have never wavered since. It was just one of those things where you just know. Sometimes there's kind of an epiphany. For me, it was two epiphanies: one at age seven, and then again at age nineteen. So, yes, to answer your question, dance and dance anthropology is all of the above for me, a passion, the dedication, all of it.

Q: What have been some of the landmark events in your dance/dance-anthropology life, and who were or are some of the major influences or inspirations in your life?

JK: Well, of course there was my mother. She was a most amazing person! She taught me Irish jigging, Spanish dancing, castanet playing, *gypsy* dancing. My mother and my father danced at the PTA doing minuets and *gypsy* dancing, and all those things, and she would teach them to me.

I also took ballet in fourth, fifth, and sixth grades. It wasn't until high school that I actually had my first modern dance classes. We had a gym teacher who had taken some classes in modern dance. So, these were some of my dance experiences.

When I went to Northwestern University, I encountered Herskovits, and that started my formal anthropology studies. And then I took a second course in anthropology shortly after the first one with Herskovits. I was still an undergraduate. It was a course in what they still called *primitive* something. It wasn't primitive religion, but primitive *something*. The course was taught by William Bascom, another famous anthropologist. So, I went in and I told him what it was that I wanted to do, and he said, "Wait a minute, let me go get Mel." And he went next door to get Herskovits. Herskovits came in and he put his arms around me, and he said, "My child, we've been waiting for *you* for a long time."

So Herskovits and Bascom were terribly important to me.

And then I met my husband, a Hawaiian. So naturally I wanted to write my dissertation on something that had to do with the Pacific, but I didn't know exactly what. So at Northwestern, we—Herskovits, Bascom, and I—cooked up a very interesting scheme. It sounds so weird now, but in some places you go for a Ph.D. and you get the master's sort of automatically. But at that time and maybe still, Northwestern didn't grant two consecutive graduate degrees. If you got your master's degree at Northwestern, you couldn't get your Ph.D. there. And so, Bascom and Herskovits wanted me to bypass the master's and just go on for the Ph.D. But I didn't want to do it on Africa only and that was Northwestern's specialty. I wanted to do it on something in the Pacific and I thought that maybe the University of Hawaii would start a Ph.D. program, which they didn't have then.

So, I wrote my master's thesis for Northwestern, but I didn't defend it or put it through or anything. Then I went to Hawaii with my husband and was gone for six years. The idea was if I could get a Ph.D. at the University of Hawaii, then they'd just put the master's through at Northwestern and I'd be done with Northwestern. If I couldn't, then I could come back to Northwestern and go on for my Ph.D., integrating the M.A. degree at Northwestern into the Ph.D.

That was the plan in 1958, but a lot of things changed in the next few years. Because, to backtrack a moment, during my graduate studies at Northwestern, two other people had become terribly important in my life: another professor, Alan Merriam, and Gertrude Kurath. Merriam was an ethnomusicologist who took over for Richard Waterman, a very famous anthropologist at the time, known, among other things, for an article that he wrote in which he brought up the question of whether a definition of dance can exist, because of the problem of language, using his studies of the Australian Aborigine as a reference point.

I met Merriam in the following way: In 1955, I returned to begin my graduate studies at Northwestern. I'd been married by this time two or three years and had gotten my undergraduate degree there the previous year and was ready to go on for my master's. So I arrived at Northwestern that fall and called Richard on the phone and told him, "I'm here." And he said, "Now, Joann, I'm sorry to tell you, but I'm leaving. I'm going to Wayne State up in Michigan. But," he said, "one of my students, a man named Alan Merriam, has just completed a lot of fieldwork in Central Africa and he's a very good person, and he's going to teach my classes."

Q: You were crestfallen?

JK: Well, the thing was that there wasn't really anybody to study with at that time and I was inventing...well, I thought I was inventing everything, you know. And so my one specific mentor was leaving, and Alan Merriam came in and did, in fact, inherit all of Richard's classes. The first class I went into had nothing to do with ethnomusicology. It was called "primitive education." And Alan starts out with a question that none of us could answer. Well, he got so angry, he threw the podium across the room and said, "When we meet the next time everybody has to have Tyler's definition of anthropology memorized and have it in exactly the right order or you're out of this class," and he stormed out.

Well, I was sort of stunned. On top of that, Edward Crowley, an anthropologist who did a huge amount of research and writing in folklore, called me shortly after school started and said, "You know, I'm not sure whether you really want to work with Alan Merriam, because he doesn't think women should be anthropologists, and I don't think that's going to be good." I said, "Well, I guess I'll just have to take that as a challenge, because he's the only game in town."

So, I went to see that man every day we had classes. For four days of every week, I went to talk with him. He'd give me something to read, I'd read it that night, and I'd go back the next day. So, finally, how could he not pay some sort of attention to me? [*laughs*] Eventually, he told me, "You know, Joann, I have to tell you the truth. I'm really not very interested in dance. I know it's important, but I'm just not interested in it." And I said, "Well, what were they doing while you were making all those sound recordings in Central Africa? I mean what were the people *doing*? And he said, "I really don't know. I wanted to make recordings out of the music, so I was spending all my time doing this and that, checking the dials and all that. My wife was taking pictures, so she can tell you what they were doing, but I really don't know."

So that really was even more of a challenge for me. I had to find out somehow. After I'd been picking his brain, he realized that I was a serious scholar and he became interested in my inquiry. 'Cause I was asking good, logical questions and really putting him through

Courtesy of Joann Keali'inohomoku

Joann in front of the totem pole at the Chicago Art Institute, 1934

his paces as well. And to everything I said, he'd find some thinking that was wrong with it. He'd say, "Well, that could describe a sport," or "That could be a religious ritual," or "That could be about a disease," or "I need to know how you are defining dance, so that it's neither too inclusive, nor too exclusive."

Well, after that year of study with Merriam, I went to Hawaii and was gone for six years between 1958 and 1964, trying to find out "what is dance?" In Hawaii I saw and experienced dance from all over Polynesia, Micronesia, Melanesia. I saw everything because I was rigorously trying to figure out how to answer that question: What is dance? How can you define it? Because the definitions that were in dictionaries were so puny, you know, it would say something like "graceful movement of the feet." [*amused chuckle*]

Ultimately I had to become circular. Something becomes *dance* because the people whose culture it is think it's dance. [*laughs*] You know, that just sounds so silly, but it's cultural. If you have a group of people and they say that what they're doing is dancing, and then you have a missionary or somebody who comes in and asks, "You call *that* dance?" Then, you see, you've got the idea of ethnocentricity and values and all those sorts of things to consider. Ultimately it comes down to the idea of being *emic* rather than *etic*.[1] [*pause*] That's all big thinking…but basic.

Q: Getting back to when you started working with Alan Merriam. He really challenged you?

JK: Yes, he challenged me, but then he said to me that he didn't know anything about dance anthropology but that there was this woman who was a member of the Society for Ethnomusicologists and that he thought I should get in touch with her. So he gave me Gertrude Kurath's name and address and I wrote to her. And that summer, which was…oh, my God!… the summer of '56! I went up to Ann Arbor and did a tutorial with her.

She wasn't an anthropologist per se, but she was studying the dances as would an anthropologist. She was brilliant. She had studied in Germany and was *beautifully* educated. She had begun to systematically work with dance while studying Iroquois dancing. Then she took an extended trip to Mexico and started working with different kinds of groups down in Mexico, the Yaqui and other groups. Up in Michigan, when I worked with her, she was studying the Holiness Church and the powwows, and all of those things. So she single-handedly invented a way of studying these Indians.

She knew labanotation, but she felt that it wasn't useful for the field, because labanotation is valuable when you can see something done over and over and over again. But if you're in the field, sometimes you can't even have a pencil in your hand while you're watching. So she started to develop a kind of shorthand, a glyph system influenced by labanotation. So during the summer I was with her, she taught me how to do that. It was wonderful to be able to actually go to these places with her and then talk about them.

Q: So, when you go to a dance as a dance anthropologist, what happens? Do you simply watch?

JK: Most of the time, yeah.

Q: And what's the first thing you look at? How does it work? Because it is such a specialized way of looking at dance. It just occurred to me that we could do this entire interview talking about who influenced you, but not talk about what it is you actually do as a dance anthropologist. What is it?

JK: I look at the *entire* event. Of course, the term "dance event" is big now. But, actually, I think I was the first to coin the term to be used with dance in this context. And when I'm talking about a dance event, I'm talking about the entire dance culture. When they plan it, the reason why it's happening, when they talk about it ahead of time, how all of it is being worked out. And then, I guess you would say, I'm just like a hungry sponge. [*laughs*] I try to remember everything in terms of all of my senses. The whole ambiance of the event: if it's in the day or at night, the balance of the environment, the temperature, the people who are there, not only the ones who are dancing but all of the people involved. Of course, I try to remember the movement, the costumes, and so on, but also I try to overhear everything that's being said, with the feeling tone and the reason why they are saying it.

I've become so accustomed to being in places where I couldn't take notes that I've trained myself to do what I call "memory ethnography" where I'm always trying to find little hooks, mnemonic aids to help me remember. But also, whenever it's possible (and it's one of the things that I've been able to do with the Hopi and the Hawaiians, and the Yaqui particularly), I just go back again and again and again and again and again. Because every time you go, you get a deeper knowledge, a deeper feeling about something. You can't just have a questionnaire, you know. I mean you can have that, too, but when you talk with people and they can say, "Oh, do you remember two years ago when we did it?" and you hear what they're saying, what *they* think is important, what *they* remember as being good or bad, or what *they* wish was different or something like that, you know, it's a different thing. So all of this is feeding into it, and feeding into it, and feeding into it, until you feel like you are just immersed in it.

And, of course, one of the goals for ethnostudies is to try to learn enough so that if you were in that culture, you'd be able to function. And maybe you are never really going to be able to try it out, but it's sort of in your mind that, you know, "If I were really living here and these were *my* people, *my* background and *my* roots, how would I feel about this? What do I *see*? What do I *think*? What is the *vocabulary* that is being used? How do I *anticipate*? How do I *remember*?" It's very big!

Q: Wow, it's huge! And Kurath gave you the beginning tools to start doing this? She was a big influence in that way?

JK: Yes, she was. And one of her major contributions to the field was that she gave an impetus to the ethnomusicologists of the time who realized that you can't know about music without knowing about dance.

Q: So what were some of the major challenges you faced along your journey? And what were some of the choices you had to make? Were there difficult ones? Are there choices that stand out as exceptionally good ones? Looking at them now, would you make different ones?

JK: One of the biggest challenges right from the very beginning, even when I was going to college, was that you don't always have a Herskovits or a Bascom or Merriam who are always with you. They understood what I was trying to do. But most other people didn't. And I was always kind of falling between the cracks, because the dance people thought that anybody who was going to be an anthropologist would be cold and unfeeling. And there were a lot of anthropologists who, still to this day, feel that dance doesn't have anything to do with anthropology. So that was, and still is, a big challenge for me.

However, the situation in the dance community has changed a lot, because in the last few years, there've been a lot of people in dance getting degrees in anthropology and stuff like this. So that has changed considerably. But I think there are still a lot of people who think they understand the content, but they're still not understanding the dance theory behind it. I mean, a lot of theories come and go. But, I'm talking about the kind of theory that's going to be lasting. For example, you might have somebody in a dance department, and they suddenly decide that they really should have a course on world culture. Well, they haven't a clue. And so they put together something. Well, I don't know, I mean I suppose on the one hand a person can argue it's better that they have something than nothing.

Q: And you believe this is continuing to get better?

JK: Well, at least it's not the same as it used to be. You know, for a long time the only thing you saw in university classes was modern dance. And they very often didn't want even the more progressive modern forms like Erick [Hawkins]. Department after department wanted Western concert dance. Then there was that long period of time when they had the so-called primitive dance. That was during the sixties and seventies. And then you would have some outside teachers who might come in and teach something like flamenco. Now they might have some form of African dance. But they don't really have it seriously as part of the curriculum to include Javanese dance, let's say. One of the first groups that really started doing that was the Dance Ethnology Program at UCLA. And what they did was very, very, very important. But as I see it now, in almost any place I go, if I tell a dance person in CORD [Congress on Research in Dance] or any place like that that I'm an anthropologist, they understand. But believe me, for a long time, it was, "What?"

For example, to use my article of 1965, "An Anthropologist Looks at Ballet," well-known scholars in the dance field to this day have remarked about me, "Oh, well, she's really nice, you know. Even though she must *hate* ballet or she couldn't call it ethnic dance." [*giggles*] But I have beautiful memories of ballet from my childhood at the World's Fair and all that. But since that article, there are people who think that I don't like ballet. That's crazy! Of course I do. I just love *dance!* All of it—all kinds—and it includes ballet. But because of my background I see that there is so much more than just ballet, that all dance is of equal value. And to me, ballet is just as important as flamenco or Kabuki or whatever. And if you're going to call *them* ethnic, meaning that they reflect their own culture, which, of course, they do, then how can you not call ballet ethnic?

Q: Right.

JK: I mean that was my basic point. But I never had the idea that this means that I don't like ballet. Yet many people still say, "Oh, you! Why do you hate ballet?" I never said that! Funny that to this day that article is still controversial. I can't believe it.

Q: So, with all of these challenges that you have encountered through your life, what were your responses? Did they divert you or were they part of what you were doing?

JK: Some of the choices I've made I believe I mentioned earlier, but one of the things that makes it hard is that I don't have enough money. I never have enough money. I was at the university for fourteen years, which was good. But I decided that I really had to devote myself to this place [Cross-Cultural Dance Resources]. I didn't become an anthropologist to be a teacher at a university. I really wanted to do my research and so on. But, fortunately, university teaching did give me a small income, so I've been able to survive. But everything that comes in, I put into this place. And that's not a complaint. That's just the truth. I mean, I have a good life. I live in a beautiful atmosphere. I'm surrounded by my books. I just hope I live long enough to get some of this stuff done. That's all. So money has always felt like an obstacle.

Q: And what are some of the major ideas you would want to relate to dancers or dance scholars or dance anthropologists trying to survive and thrive in the dance world? What would you like to tell them?

JK: Well, I should go back to the idea of following your passion. I'm sure that everybody you're talking to probably is saying that also. Maybe not. You know, when you've lived as many years as I have, you can be sure that over the years, there have been lots of times when things were one way or the other. Maybe they weren't necessarily the way you would choose or sometimes they would open up in amazing ways. I mean good, bad, and indifferent, you know, there are going to be all kinds of things as we follow our journey of life. It happens to everybody. But I think the fact that I was able to find something that I really believe in has just carried me through everything. And I don't know whether you can tell that to somebody else, because if they don't have that passion, how can they get it? How can you tell them?

[*pause*]

Q: And do you see a significant trend in any aspect of your field in dance anthropology, either in the training of it or in the attitudes of people both in and out of the field or in the subject matter being studied? Are there trends or common things that you see?

JK: Yeah, I'll take the example of two different dance anthropologists; they may exemplify others in the field. Both of the anthropologists I have in mind have been very concerned about this whole definition thing to the point where they don't even want to use the word "dance" anymore. So that's why one doesn't even use the word "dance" in her descriptions and discussions. She uses "human movement." Well, I find that not acceptable. I mean you and I are doing human movement right now as we sit here and I think that's something worth studying. But you know, when you add other ideas of affectivity and so on…well, you lose something if you simply call it human movement.

And the other anthropologist doesn't want to use the word "dance" much anymore either, although she belongs to the ethnochoreologists. What she calls it is "structured movement." Well, I just don't find that very satisfying either. In both cases they're studying dance, they're talking about dance, so why these other terms? This is actually a fieldwide issue. We had a symposium last summer, and Allegra Fuller Snyder was our keynote speaker. It was one of the points that she brought up: she is worried about whether dance is going to get lost in these other studies.

I think a lot of people, in an attempt to be holistic and put things in larger contexts, sometimes begin to veer away. So, I don't know… it'll be interesting to see where it goes.

Q: And your dreams for the future and for the field?

JK: Well…first of all I have to publish a lot of the articles that I've written before, as a collection. I think it's important, because I realize that a lot of the things that I wrote, people haven't read.

Q: That would be great. They're not all in one place and they're hard to find.

JK: They are hard to find, so that's one thing that I have to get done. However, another thing is that back in the sixties, I did some very important interviews with a woman named Jenny Wilson, who was a Hawaiian. I think I can show you her picture. [*shows photograph*] She was the last living court dancer for King David Kalakaua, the last king of Hawaii And she was the one who brought the hula to the mainland back in 1893.

Another thing that I really have to do is complete the work I've been doing with signatures[2] and silhouettes.

Q: These are movement signatures? Or is it more complex than that?

JK: Well, it's more complex than that. Actually, the whole idea about the silhouettes or the *silhougraphs*, as I call them now, started when I was a graduate student and one of my professors asked me to come and speak to his linguistics class. He said he wanted me to talk about movement and dancing, because they all had trained their ears, but they didn't know how to train their eyes.

So I was trying to think how I could make people's eyes focus, for example, if they saw a slide or something. So I thought, "Well, I'll just fill in a figure." And the first one I did was of José Greco. And it just *jumped* out at me. There was no movement, no "in-motion" movement. There was no sound. There were no three-dimensions, there was no color, there was no nothing, but I knew immediately what it was. So I was asking myself, "What is encoded in that thing that I can read it?" How is it that a person can draw an outline of two figures, say, for a square dance Saturday, and everybody knows by looking at it it's going to be a square dance? *Why do they know that?*

So I've been working on that now since the sixties. I've got thousands of these *silhougraphs*. Of course, the computers could do it, too, but they don't really do it exactly right, because they're still working with bytes and bits and pixels and stuff, so it's not quite the same as doing it by hand. The rigor of doing my *silhougraphs* is that I copy them exactly. The fact that I'm doing it by hand, as I go through it, I'm learning an awful lot. You know, it's a wonderful learning experience about what those bodies are really doing. Where is the balance and all that sort of thing. And then when you have several of them, it really stands out in your mind what the context and the contrast are, the comparative study of them. Why is it that we're able to look at something and know that this is Javanese, or that's Ghanian? Why do we know that? What are we looking at?

Well, maybe we're told, and maybe we hear the music, and we see the movement, but there's something else. It's one of the reasons why I feel that labanotation isn't sufficient, because it shows the movement, which, of course, is important. But it doesn't tell you what the phenotype of the human being is. For example, if you have a Mohave woman, who's in this very specific dress, the space is being shaped by what she's wearing and not just by the way she's moving.

We all know that you move according to what you're wearing and what you're carrying. So, that's why I decided I would look for a word. If you have the word "graph," like a photograph or a pictograph, it indicates that it is a direct copying. So I combine "silho," which is the blackening of it, with "graph" and call them "silhougraphs." I have, in fact, registered that name.

Q: And what do you wish for your field? What do you want in the future for a younger generation of people in the dance field?

JK: Hmmm, it sounds so corny to say it, but I would just love it if people could start looking out of the box, you know? This is one of the things that I've tried to do. I try to see things, look at things, hear things freshly. I think there's so much that we can learn about human beings, about cultures, if people could just be fresh. That would be my wish. Also, if they could see that dance is affective, that it is important, that it's part of this larger thing, you know. I just think that the *whole* is going to be very small if people can't build on it.

Q: Um, you mentioned the term "affective" a few times. Dance as being *affective*. How do you define affective?

JK: Affective means it moves you. But I don't see *emotion* as being a total synonym. I think in the Bible it says, "Man does not live by bread alone." Human beings aren't content to just eat, sleep, screw, shit, all that sort of thing. They have to have something that they look forward to, something they make a sacrifice for, something that moves them. We live with things like that all the time, you know, the way you decorate your house, or the flag goes by and you stand up, all that stuff. The flag is just a piece of cloth, but it goes beyond symbolism into the idea of signatures. Symbolism doesn't make you move, but a signature does. And it ties in with a notion of affectivity. So when people dance, they're going beyond what their ordinary everyday activity is. And somehow, it's meaningful to them, to their society, to their friends, or whatever it is. All human beings have to have something that makes life worth living and dance fits into that category. It is something that moves you.

A well-known British biologist once said, "We ignore the arts and the dance and music at our peril." This fits right into the idea of dance being a human universal. If we didn't have it, humans wouldn't continue to procreate. It's adaptive. Through it we have a sense of history, we have a sense of anticipation, and we have a sense of beauty, we have a sense of why. Why does every group have something that is an ideal, a religion, an ethics? Those are human characteristics. I can't think of any other creature, except there may be some that we don't now know of, maybe dolphins have an entirely different kind of affective culture that we just don't understand yet. But so far as we're able to know, this is a very human kind of thing to do. Also, our ability to make choices is another thing that distinguishes us from all of the other animals. You see, when people start saying, "Oh, well, you see those birds? They're dancing." No, no, no! Or the "Rain Dance of the Chimpanzees" or something like that. No! They don't sit down and say, "Now we need to practice this, and the last time we did it we did it too fast, so the next time we're going to do it slower," or "We're going to invent a whole new way of moving and let's try partnering, and let's try doing it in a solo…" I mean, it's only humans that do that.

Q: And you find that this happens even in some of the more, *primitive* situations you've seen?

JK: Absolutely. Absolutely.

Keali'inohomoku as a resident scholar at the School of American Research in Santa Fe, NM, circa 1975

Q: Well, we're almost finished, but here is another question that is a little off the map here, but I think it's very pertinent to your work. Is there a dance event that you can talk about, or some dance ritual you might have seen, that has been a highlight for you? What was the place? What was the temperature? What was one of the more memorable dances that you have witnessed that really *affected* you?

JK: Oh, that would be the Yaqui Deer Dance! The dance itself has an X-quality, you know, where you can either have good dancers or bad dancers. But the dance itself is something that stands on its own.

JK: I first saw it in 1971, and I was just dumbfounded. It's a single dance for one man. It's done at a particular time during the Easter period. It can be done during the day or at night.

[*pause*]

The deer dancer is a single dancer. He is a deer dancer because he dreamed he is going to be a deer dancer, and so he apprentices himself and he learns how to do it. And then there are two, three, or four different people who dance with him. But they don't perform the same kind of dance. They're called *pascolas* and they have a mask, which sometimes is on their face, and sometimes is on the side of their head. When it's on the side of their head, they're doing a kind of jiggy dance, because they're acting as the hosts of the festival. But at a certain time, when they receive a signal from their drummer, then the mask goes in front of the face, and they become kind of animals.

Some of the stories say that they're sons of the devil who live in a special kind of world. Now the Yaqui have several different kinds of traditional worlds and the Flower World is where these magic animals live. And so the deer with his mask and through his dreaming enters the Flower World.

And there are four musicians. One of them sits cross-legged. He holds the drum and plays the flute at the same time. That's the pascolas music when they're dancing with the deer. And then there's a kind of a rug. There are three guys sitting on *that*. They are deer singers. One is scraping, in fact, two are making a scraping sound, one is hitting a half gourd with a string on it in a pan of water, so you hear the sound of that. The hitting is the deer's heart, and the scraping is the breath he's trying to catch. So they sing songs that have to do with whatever animals are out at that time: whatever insects, whatever birds and so on. But they're singing it in Yaqui. And the one who's playing the flute and the drum is playing an entirely separate song. And they all happen simultaneously. It's so fantastic.

Q: How do people know that the Deer Dance will happen? Do they collect to witness it? What is the setting?

JK: Well, yes, people collect to see it. Usually it's done in kind of a ramada that's set up especially for it. So if the whole place is like a plaza and you have all kinds of things going on, then there'll be this little ramada that'll probably be the size of maybe this room [approximately 12' x 15'] with a little fence around it and people stand next to the fence and watch.

The deer and the pascolas are inside, and the deer wears a cloth over his head, so it's kind of down over his eyes. You don't see his regular eyes and he has a head of a deer on the top. And he doesn't put that on until the *very last* second. When the deer is not dancing, the guy who's the deer stays there with his arms folded.

Sometimes they're young and sometimes they're old. There are four Yaqui villages in Tucson and each one has their own deer dancers. I've seen some of the classic ones who got to be very, very old, but there are some young ones that are coming along.

I've been looking at this dance since 1971, and every time I've seen it, the deer, no matter what his age, stays there with his arms folded waiting 'til it's his turn. So when you hear that drum—da-da-da-da-da-da-da—then you know that the pascolas are transforming from entertainers into the animals that will be chasing and trying to track down the deer.

And then the scraping sound starts. So you've got that with the da-da-da-da-da-da-da in the drum. Then the flute begins, and then one of the guys comes out and he's looking around, trying to find the deer. And the deer is still standing there like this. [*folds her arms*]

And then, just at the last second, the deer dancer ties a scarf on his head. He acts like he's got forever. You think he's never going to get there in time. He puts this thing on his head and ties it, and he's *so slow*. And you think [*whispers*], "Hurry up! Hurry up! Hurry up!"

And he picks up a rattle in his hand. And you can *see* the transformation. He comes up. He shakes like this [*shakes head with chin slightly down*]…and you watch the head…and you see the deer is in the forest, and it's looking from left to right. And then, one-at-a-time, these pascolas will dance at him—not with him—but at him.

The whole idea is that they're trying to chase him down. But he's a different deer. He's the magic faun. And each time the deer does slightly different movements according to what different kinds of animals are out. But the movements are not imitative of the deer; they're the essence of deer. And at midnight, there are different kinds of crickets and birds than there are at one o'clock and at two o'clock in the morning, so the songs are reflective of that.

And you look at this and you say, "I just never saw anything so exquisite in my life." It's just so *wonderful* you just can't believe it! And then in the morning time, after they've been singing and dancing all night long, the guy who's got the water drum, well, he throws the water out like this. [*Flinging gesture toward the ground*]

And if you didn't know what he was doing, you wouldn't realize it, but what he's done is he's made a cross on the ground. Because all of this water has been sung and danced over all these hours, and so it's become sacred. By the time you've arrived at morning, it's holy water. You know, the whole thing is just so, so rich. A person can walk in without having any idea of what is going on and they would still be thrilled. But, as you get to know more and more and more, you feel and hear yourself expanding. I don't know. It's like you've put some little dried thing in a pan of water and it begins to swell. That's what my reaction is like.

You know, through all of these years, I've had so many wonderful things like this that I've been able to see and to be privy to, that I feel like I'm just so filled with it all.

NOTES

1. According to Keali'inohomoku, "emic frames are subjective points of view by participants in the culture as well as by individual scholars who are researching selective dance cultures. Conversely, etic frames are objective points of view that researchers employ to study phenomena comparatively. Interaction between emic and etic views facilitate holistic interpretation and fundamentally define the process of cross-cultural or comparative dance study."

2. According to Keali'inohomoku, "the Doctrine of Signatures has a long written history going back to the Middle Ages. It is more popularly understood as sympathetic magic or homeopathy. Those terms seem old-fashioned and discredited, but my own research has shown it to be an important concept embedded in the belief systems of diverse peoples. Our own society is filled with signatures and sympathetic magic but of course not so labeled. For example, a thumbprint is a signature. A snowflake has its own signature. It is a sticky subject and easily misunderstood, but I have realized it is a key to understanding people's worldviews. A silhourgraph is a complex of signatures. A certain shape can be 'read' to identify a dance, a particular person, and a type of costume."

Photo by James Black

Bill Evans

BILL EVAN

BILL EVANS

"I've never questioned the validity of what I do as a dance teacher, performer, or choreographer. It just seems innately noble to me."

A Utah native, performer, choreographer, and movement analyst, Bill Evans is first and foremost a dance educator who has taught dance and coordinated programs in private studios, professional training programs, K–12 schools, and higher education institutions for the past fifty years. Having trained with some of the world's leading dance masters, including Willam Christensen, Jack Cole, Viola Farber, José Limón, Matt Mattox, Donald McKayle, Daniel Nagrin, and Anna Sokolow (to name only a few), Evans went on to create the Bill Evans Dance Company and two tap ensembles, enjoying critical success for over thirty years. He has performed and presented his work in all fifty states, throughout Canada and Mexico, and in Australia, England, Finland, France, Germany, Hungary, India, Italy, Ireland, Japan, New Zealand, Norway, and Russia. Full-time and guest professorships have included positions with the University of Utah, the University of Washington, Indiana University, and the University of New Mexico. He is currently a visiting professor/guest artist in the Dance Department at the State University of New York [SUNY-Brockport]. Evans has been awarded the Guggenheim Fellowship, numerous grants and fellowships from the National Endowment for the Arts, and more than seventy other awards from public and private arts agencies in the United States and Canada, including National Dance Association Scholar/Artist of the Year (1997), New Mexico Governor's Award for Excellence in the Arts (2001), and the National Dance Education Organization's Lifetime Achievement Award (2005). Evans holds a bachelor of arts in English and ballet and an MFA in modern dance from the University of Utah (Salt Lake City). He is both a certified movement and certified Laban/Bartenieff movement analyst.

SETTING THE SCENE

Similar to the trail that led me to Carolyn Carlson, my journey toward meeting Bill Evans first began in 1991 during a teaching tour out West. Almost every dancer I met from the West had been influenced by Bill. Surrounded by the sparkling austerity of the New Mexican desert, Bill opened his home and life to me at a point of change. Within the next few weeks, he would begin a new adventure in Brockport, New York, after sixteen years in New Mexico. The thoughtfulness and candor with which he answered the interview questions created a reflective stillness around us. We sat over the course of the late morning and better portion of the afternoon, gazing at the beautiful desert outside his windows as he revisited moments and meaning in his life.

— R.C.

Q: The first question I have for you is, if you were in a group of children, or a group of nondancers, how would you describe your work to them?

BE: Well, for many years now, I've described myself as a university professor. So, that's how I'd start. Then they'd want to know what I teach, so I'd say, "Dance." That's usually startling to people. Boys and adults of both sexes often seem uncomfortable knowing this. From my early childhood, I'd say, "I'm a dancer," and I'd see people recoil a little and say, "What?" [*pause*] There is a disquieting prejudice in our culture against dancers, especially male dancers.

A more accurate answer to your question would be, "I'm a teacher, choreographer, and performer."

What I'd really like people to know is that my work is focused around multiple aspects of the study of movement, which is life itself, and which includes dance, the most direct manifestation of the human spirit. My work is about exploring, confirming, and celebrating the ways in which life is a process of continuous, exciting, and delicious change. To me, dance is not separate from life, but is at the very heart of life itself. I really do believe that.

Q: Do you consider your involvement with dance to be your profession? Is it your career, your work, your passion, your calling? Is it all of the above?

BE: Yes, all of the above. I knew when I was three years old that dance was my calling. My family lived in Salt Lake City until I was five. My mother's youngest sister took me to the first film I had ever seen (in a Mormon ward house) when I was three years old, and in that film some guy was tap dancing. Well, I went home and immediately started making up my own tap dances. I held marbles under my toes to make sounds on the concrete basement floor. The fact that I needed to dance was just very clear to me. It didn't come with cerebral content, of course. I simply started doing it. And my life just unfolded around dancing, and I've been dancing ever since.

I think I'm very fortunate that I was able to find my bliss at a very, very early age. So yes, it is my calling.

It's also my job. Except for two years in the army, I've never made money except as a dancer, dance teacher, or choreographer. In fact, I started teaching as a teenager and have supported myself since age thirteen. So, yes, it's a job. However, it is certainly my passion. If it were not my job, I would do it anyway, because it fulfills me. So, yes, it's all of the above.

Q: How did you first get introduced to dance? What are some of the landmark events in your dance life and who were or are some of your major influences?

BE: My aunt Dorothy started taking tap lessons when I was about four. When I saw her do *flap ball change* in her patent leather shoes and blue taffeta dress with a big bow, I started pestering my parents to let me take lessons, too. Finally, when I was eight and a half, my father reluctantly gave up his resistance to the idea and enrolled me in the combined tap and ballet classes of Charles Purrington, a retired vaudevillian hoofer who had settled in Salt Lake City and established the Purrington Academy of Dance Art. Soon I advanced to the classes of his daughter June Purrington Park, who had danced in Hollywood with Ernest Belcher, Marge Champion's father, and Louis DaPron, who taught and choreographed for moving picture dance stars and performed in films himself.

To this day, June Park is the teacher who has inspired me the most. She had a wonderful dignity about her and, even though her aesthetic sensibilities were developed in Hollywood, she had a remarkable elegance and crafted classes of remarkable musicality and structural integrity. She was a classically trained pianist and accompanied all her own classes on a baby grand. This was in Salt Lake City. We had moved to my father's hometown, the historic Mormon village of Lehi, by then, and we commuted more than an hour each way, traversing the Point of the Mountain, a stretch of highway that was often treacherous in wintertime.

At age fifteen, I started to study with Willam Christensen, founder of the San Francisco Ballet, in the extension division of the ballet program at the University of Utah. He also inspired me, but in a very different way. He was a macho, powerful, and dynamic force. He worked furiously, with remarkable *passion*. I looked at him as a model of how one can accomplish something seemingly impossible if one is determined, believes in himself, and doesn't give up. By the time I graduated from the University of Utah, I had studied with him and Gordon Paxman, his assistant, for eight years. Actually, he and I never quite saw eye to eye on many things. He was quite a homophobe, and so many of the young men who danced for him had to pretend that they were hypermasculine to advance in his company.

Q: And you were out about your sexuality?

BE: No, I wasn't out or even aware, but I was effeminate. I was in denial, trying to believe that I was heterosexual. But he recognized things in me that were clearer to everyone else than they were to me, and, as a result, he kept me at a distance. His reservations weren't about my talent. They were about who I was when I wasn't dancing. But anyway, I'm very grateful for all he taught me. I developed extraordinary physical strength when I was dancing with him. He conducted special men's classes, and at the time I was studying with him, Michael Smuin, Kent Stowell, Finis Jhung, Jamie DeBolt, and a number of other very gifted men who were about my age were also his students. He pushed us incredibly hard and we developed phenomenal strength and skill.

Years later, in the early seventies, he supported my development as a choreographer and invited me to make two ballets for Ballet West. Truth is, I ended up really loving the guy, and I revere him.

I didn't know there was such a thing as modern dance until my freshman year at the University of Utah. My friend Emily Roberts and I had developed a little jazz dance act...and one day she said, "Come to the Orchesis audition." This was December of my freshman year at the university. So, she and I went to the audition and performed a jazz routine that we had choreographed together. Well, Shirley Ririe and Joan Woodbury, directors of Orchesis (and now of the Ririe-Woodbury Dance Company), said, "Your piece is not really choreography because it just consists of two people doing the same thing from beginning to end." This idea was new to me. However, they saw a young man who was strong and coordinated [*laughs*] and they immediately and enthusiastically wanted me to start dancing with them, which I did. I didn't really study modern dance as an official student, but I attended their technique classes whenever I could, and I performed in their student and preprofessional companies for five years.

Q: And what was their technique? Did they use improv?

BE: They loved improv. Improvisation *was* very important to them, and very difficult for me in the beginning. They taught eclectic technique. Shirley and Joan were quite different, but each included a little bit of Graham, Humphrey/Limón, Holm and Nikolais, with a touch of Tamiris in her technique classes. Of course, I didn't know then what it was we were studying. I was simply in awe of their seemingly endless stores of movement knowledge.

Of course, Bill Christensen would call me in to his office after ballet classes, which I took as an official student, and tell me that "those crazy ladies" didn't know what they were doing.

Q: Of course.

BE: But my instinct told me that he just didn't understand. They had something that I was very much interested in, and so I was the only male who was then both a ballet and a modern dancer at the University of Utah. At that time, modern dance was in the Women's Physical Education Department and ballet was in the Department of Speech and Theatre. For one semester, I ventured into the modern dance major because I saw women who were graduating with their bachelor's degrees in P.E. with an emphasis in modern dance and getting jobs like that [*snaps fingers*] in universities. And I thought, "Wouldn't that be the life?" So I tried the physical education major for one quarter but it was just too uncomfortable. You couldn't be just a P.E. major, you had to be a *women's* P.E. major, and people looked at me really strangely when I had to proclaim my major, and I was too insecure to ignore them, so I gave up on the modern dance emphasis but continued to dance with Shirley and Joan.

They inspired me enormously for many of the same reasons as Bill Christensen. They were uncompromising in their determination to follow their passion despite any resistance. They worked endlessly, and they were inspiring and tough and astonishingly successful.

I don't think any of them (Bill, Shirley, or Joan) were artistic models so much as role models for being dedicated and determined and having a vision and bringing it to life.

So then, I went into the army after graduation and then I moved to New York. Ahh, while in the army, I was in a tank accident and I crushed the talus, one of the tarsals, of my left foot and developed a condition known as aseptic necrosis, death without infection. For seven and a half months, I could put no weight on my left foot, and when the bones finally recalcified, they had reconfigured so that when one looks at an X-ray of my left ankle and foot, the size and shape of the bones are almost unrecognizable. Well, as soon as I was able to, I started moving again, I started walking again, I started dancing again, and I went through a long period where my ankle had almost no mobility, but I was dancing on it. And ten years later, in 1973, when I was thirty-three, I was taking an RDT [Repertory Dance Theatre] class with Matt Mattox and we all heard this tremendous snap! No pain whatsoever! And in an instant most of the mobility returned to my ankle. I guess the scar tissue that had been there for ten years just finally gave up.

Q: Amazing…

BE: So anyway, when I went to New York in 1965 after the army, because of my ankle condition, I thought, "Well, I won't be a ballet dancer or a modern dancer, but I'll be a musical theater dancer because I won't have to push the ankle so much." But I never got around to that because I had been in New York for just a few days when my friend Mariano Parra (who had a Spanish dance company in the Village), took me over to introduce me to Robert Joffrey, who gave me a scholarship. He looked at my foot and nonetheless, somehow, figured, "Well, it's worth taking a chance on him." And then, about a month later, I was taking a class from William Griffith at Ballet Theatre and I was standing next to the New York City Ballet principal dancer, Patricia Wilde, at the barre, and at the end of the class she said, "Would you like to come over to the Harkness House for Ballet Arts?" Pat had just become director of the professional training program there. Rebekah Harkness, Joffrey's former patroness, had decided to take his dancers, who were under personal contract to her, and start her own company, featuring her very tall boyfriend. Bob Scevers was 6'4" and he looked strange surrounded by all the amazing but rather short former Joffrey dancers…Helgi Tomasson, Finis Jhung, Larry Rhodes, Lone Isaksen I mean, these were all incredibly skilled and beautiful dancers, but they were small. So she wanted tall men and she sent Patricia Wilde to scout them out.

So I got this job at Harkness and it gave me food and money and clothing and medical care and classes all day long. And during my time with Harkness, I had the opportunity to study with, among others, Jack Cole. I danced from eight in the morning to five in the afternoon studying with other wonderful people: Leon Fokine, Aubrey Hitchens, Stuart Hodes, Matt Mattox, Vera Volkova, Patricia Wilde, and many others. But then after dancing all day long, I'd work with Jack Cole for two more hours, from five to seven PM. Jack had selected about a dozen dancers whom he was willing to work with for that period. It was exhilarating!

Q: How old was he at that time?

BE: He was about fifty-five. He had been in Hollywood and come back to New York. About the time I was working with him, he wanted to get back into his serious concert work, I think. So anyway, I worked with him and that was a truly remarkable experience. We were studying Bharata Natyam,[1] Cecchetti ballet, and Spanish classical dance forms with him. We studied the Humphrey/Weidman floor exercises he had learned, I guess, when he was in the Weidman company. His classes were just life changing for me.

Up to that point, I think, he had not been primarily in a teacher's role. He was a very troubled individual and consequently his primary method of teaching was humiliation. But he had an incredible kinesthetic intelligence. At fifty-five, his body was extraordinarily supple and he moved with remarkable precision and clarity of intent. He had what I call today connectivity, to a degree that I hadn't seen up to that point.

Q: Especially in a male role model?

BE: Right. Most of the men who were my teachers at that time had stopped moving. But Cole was still very much a mover and very alive in his body and he had a passion for doing things "right." And not "right" in a kind of superficial way but "right" in a deep way. Sometimes, he would teach us a phrase of eight counts and we would do that phrase over and over and over for two hours. And I thought, "Oh my God!" No one in my life had ever cared about detail that much. And while at the same time, it was maddening, it was also so eye-opening to think that one could see so deeply and care so deeply about movement.

In class he was a monster and out of class he was a gracious and compassionate man. After two hours of brutal treatment, he would often call us over and have a little tête-à-tête, or he often invited us to go with him to the New York City Ballet. We would sit there and he would say, "Now there's Violette Verdy…now that's who you should watch! Now, over there, she's a robot; look at her arms!" Or, "She's a disaster, never dance like that!" He would point out who was dancing harmoniously in her body and I started to value that. It was the first time I really came in contact with someone who honored anatomy. He gave me a concern for detail that allowed for working the human body in harmony with its structure, without pain, and he gave me the notion that one could dance for a lifetime.

After working as a professional ballet dancer for a couple of years, I went back to Utah, where I was asked to join the Repertory Dance Theatre in 1967. I stayed there until I was thirty-four. In the early days, RDT was a collective, a democracy. All twelve of us made all of our decisions by consensus. I became first the chair of the dancers' committee, and then one of three artistic coordinators, a job I held for six of my seven years in the company. I usually functioned as the artistic administrator of the company. But none of the decisions or suggestions I made could be finalized without the support of a majority of the dancers. This democratic process was both excruciatingly difficult and wonderful, because it gave everyone a sense of ownership in the process, and helped form the leadership style I follow today.

We had unbelievable opportunities in RDT because artists like José Limón and Anna Sokolow, and other really significant choreographers would come and spend four weeks at a time with us. So, our company of twelve dancers had Anna Sokolow all to ourselves, or José Limón all to ourselves, or Glen Tetley or Donald McKayle all day, every day, for a month. Their own companies in New York didn't have them like that! The kind of intensity that we experienced with those people was quite extraordinary.

In RDT, I was surrounded by these other men with phenomenal bodies: Tim Wengerd, who later became a principal male dancer in the Martha Graham Company, Manzell Senters, Erik Newton, and Gregg Lizenbery. Each had a range of motion that was unbelievable. I have a more typical male body. I don't have a lot of flexibility and I have a very long torso. So I looked at those guys and I thought, "Oh, my god, they can do so many things that I can't do." And I felt quite inadequate.

But then Sokolow worked with us and said, "But you are an artist." Ah, those magic words. She helped me realize that the intent and the passion I have for what I do and the depth and intensity with which I care about dance meant something. She created a work for us called *Steps of Silence* and I had a pivotal role in the piece. I was thrilled to have her develop it on me. And then she taught me the "Good Soldier" solo, from *Lyric Suite*. She and I became close friends and we remained connected for many years.

Betty Jones came out repeatedly. She helped me discover physical integrity as a mover and honesty as a performer. She taught me about lightness and inner shaping through a perspective that had been very influenced by Lulu Sweigard.[2] I remember we were rehearsing Limón's *Concerto Grosso* one day and she stopped us and had the other company members watch me. She called attention to the qualitative aspect of my dancing, my embodiment of free flow and lightness, the indulgent qualities in Laban's Effort work, and internal shaping and simplicity. These qualities weren't really valued by my teachers and choreographers up to that point, but she validated and celebrated them. In that way, she validated me. And so, she was a very, very important influence on my belief in myself and in my own dancing.

And then Ethel Winter became one of our major teachers. Ethel went to Martha and said, "I have the perfect cast here for *Appalachian Spring*." At that point, Martha would still not let anyone perform her works except her own company and Batsheva.[3] But she gave permission for us to learn *Appalachian Spring* and to perform it in educational settings. And Ethel Winter said to me, "You dance just like the young Erick Hawkins when he did *Appalachian Spring*." So, I got to do that role.

These artists and their mentorship gave me perspective from different points of view on what I could and couldn't do.

Q: And some of the landmark events?

BE: Well, RDT was a seven-year landmark event. I went back to Utah thinking I wouldn't stay very long, but after I had been in the company for one year, we invited Clive Barnes and Walter Terry and others to come to Salt Lake City to see us. So they did, and when they went back east, Walter Terry wrote that I was an "up-and-coming national choreographer" and Clive Barnes wrote that I was "someone to watch." Subsequently, Walter Terry wrote three or four articles for *Saturday Review* about me over the next several years, saying that I was "one of the most important choreographic voices in America today…" something like that. Well, I was thirty years old and I thought, "I am?" I had no idea. I had been dancing since I was a kid but I had never really thought of myself as a choreographer. There again, validation from Barnes and Terry, and then from Doris Hering, Deborah Jowitt, Hubert Saal, Byron Belt, and other East Coast dance critics, allowed me to see myself in a new way.

I started getting invitations from various companies around the world to go and choreograph. And while I was with RDT for those seven years, we toured for about fifteen weeks a year and we did three or four Salt Lake City seasons a year, with at least one of my works on every program. RDT gave me numerous opportunities to try my wings as a choreographer (eighteen different works, more than any other choreographer has created for that company) and to have my work seen. So, there was kind of a long run that started at RDT and then expanded as I created work on other national and international companies.

But I grew dissatisfied with the rep situation. What happens in repertory companies, at least what happened in RDT at that time, was that we had difficulty maintaining the essence of a style. A choreographer would come and work with us intensively for a while and we would grasp that style pretty clearly and deeply. But then, as time went on, it sort of merged with other styles and lost its edge. In an evening you'd see a Limón work, a Jennifer Muller work, a Sokolow work, a John Butler work, a Glen Tetley, an Evans work, and/or a Viola Farber work. They'd come at you, bump, bump, bump. But they would sort of bleed into each other, with styles becoming kind of generalized. And I grew frustrated being so unspecific and a little bit superficial.

So, I wanted to form a group of dancers devoted to my ideas about movement, who would work with me for a period of time, perhaps over years, in which we would create work as the modern pioneers had. And so, in 1975, I formed my own company and in '76 we moved from Salt Lake City to Seattle. That was another landmark for me, when we moved to Seattle.

One year after I started my company (because of all my exposure with RDT and guest residencies), we had months of bookings. In no time, I had a company that was functioning at a high level. Having a group of dancers who dedicated themselves to learning my approach to dancing and to the ideas surrounding the work and who deeply embodied them was profoundly challenging and satisfying! I had dancers from that period who stayed with me twelve, fifteen, eighteen years. That was a very different experience than my years with RDT, where I shared dancers with many other choreographers and teachers and when, every time I would go away to create work on a commission, it would be for a different set of dancers.

Sadly, I don't have the resources now to maintain a full-time company and continue *that* kind of deep work.

Q: Is it hard to find dancers who are willing to immerse themselves in your work?

BE: Today, yes. First, I can no longer pay them very well or very frequently. And there are many other aspects to this question. In my dance generation, there wasn't much company-hopping, and you were either a ballet dancer or a modern dancer.

Q: [*laughs*] Right. Or even if you were a Graham dancer, you weren't a Hawkins dancer. You weren't a Cunningham dancer.

BE: Right. When I came to New York in '65, I would go to see the Graham Company and think, "Well, they're not mortals!" These people had devoted themselves to that work for twenty, twenty-five years. I mean, my breath was just absolutely taken away because, by being willing to go back to those ideas, day in and day out, year in and year out, they had developed a heavenly depth of

Photo by Ferd Evans

Barbara Stauffer and Bill Evans in recital costumes for Hold Tight, *choreographed by June Purrington Park, 1959*

embodiment and sense of ensemble. And you can't get that depth in any discipline without being immersed in it. It's not the same as a three-week residency with someone setting repertory. In the Cunningham Company at that time, Viola Farber, Carolyn Brown, Valda Setterfield, those people were unique individuals, eccentric and brilliant! They were an artistic family who played off each other incredibly.

Q: Yes, it's a different embodiment of detail. The specificity of it.

BE: Yeah, I mean, if I were to see the Graham Company or the Cunningham Company now, it would not be at all that kind of experience because things have become more generalized and *everyone* has killer technique and you can sort of switch the dancers around and there isn't a whole lot of difference in the quality of the experience. But, you know back then, it was not just a dance style or a dance repertory, it was a set of beliefs. It was a way of life. It was a spiritual quest.

The first time Ethel Winter did a residency with RDT, she set a couple of pieces on us. And the night before the showing, we were having a little rehearsal and she danced a solo she had created decades before. She transformed in moments, before our eyes. And as I sat there, my whole body went into this response [*showing a tremor*]. It was the first time I had ever experienced that degree of emotional fullness in dancing. I didn't even know that kind of physical and emotional depth existed in dancing until I was close to it, watching Ethel day by day.

So anyway, I think people now…well, idealism is not popular. Understandably, given the hypocrisy of nearly everyone in power, it hasn't been popular for quite a long time. To honor a set of ideals and be willing to devote yourself to them, that's just a very unpopular kind of thing at the moment. I haven't even imagined for a number of years now that many dancers would be willing to work with me anymore in that way.

But anyway, the next landmark event…in 1975, my company did a month-long residency at San Jose State University. And Janet Van Swoll, the director of the program, had invited me and my new, young company to teach technique, comp, improv, and rep, and also Peggy Hackney to come and teach Effort/Shape.[4] And every day Peggy took my technique class. I would present my stuff and [*snap, snap, snap*] this woman was just embodying it like that. Usually dancers who didn't have a background in my work would come into my classes and feel lost; they would struggle, because I was asking them to use less force and tension, and more free flow, and to access more internal mobility than they were used to. It was usually a struggle for people, but she was picking up my style accurately and quickly, so I thought, "I need to know more about this woman and her movement theories."

And during the next summer, my company was in residence for six weeks at the American Dance Festival, and Peggy was teaching Effort/Shape and Irene Dowd was teaching applied kinesiology there at the same time. And Irene and Peggy took my technique class every day. We had a number of students, maybe a dozen young women, who took my class, Irene's class, and Peggy's class. And at the end of the summer we looked at them and they had made impressive positive changes in their dancing. Meanwhile, many of the other students had mostly learned to defend themselves against what seemed to be contradictory demands from me, Denise Jefferson who taught Graham technique, and Mel Wong who taught Cunningham technique. But those students had made obvious and powerful changes, physically and expressively. And we thought, "My God, something remarkable can happen when people study Effort/Shape and the Sweigard work in tandem with Evans technique!" Those things really clicked together and helped people make quantum leaps of understanding and embodiment in a short time.

At the end of that summer, Peggy said, "I want to join your company." How could I say no? So, she moved to Seattle and that was a huge landmark event in my life because she brought the Laban/Bartenieff⁵ work into my company. We didn't take formal courses with her at first. She just brought the knowledge in her body/mind into the rehearsal process. I'd give her a choreographic direction and she'd say, "Oh, I'm going to try the Dream State. See if this is what you want." So she would go into bound lightness, for example. And I'd say, "No, that's not what I want," and then she'd say, "Well, let me try the Remote State?" And then she'd explain to me in Laban terms what she was trying. "Yeah, that's it!" So I started to learn about Laban, not so much in a theoretical way as through the application of it.

And then the same thing happened with Gretchen Langstaff. She brought Irene Dowd's work to my Bill Evans Seattle Summer Institute of Dance. In '77 we started a six-week summer program in which all 300 students had to study Bartenieff Fundamentals and applied kinesiology as well as my technique. And that's still the format of my summer intensive workshops to this day.

Q: Wow, that's a perfect dance education. And artistically, are there modern dancers and/or ideas that influenced you? Because you've mentioned several times that many of your influences weren't your aesthetic models.

BE: Right. Well, artistically, I think the biggest influence on me has been the dancers in my company, Gregg Lizenbery, Debbie Poulsen, Shirley Jenkins, Jim Coleman, Don Halquist, Debbi Knapp, and others. I'm not talking artistically in terms of choreographic form and strategies, but in terms of movement realization. Gregg worked with me for eighteen years and Debbie Poulsen over about nineteen years. Debbie took her very first class with me when she was about fifteen years old. Don started dancing with me at age twenty-three and has worked with me for twenty-one years. So, a lot of what I've learned to value has come from creative investigations with those dancers and that's true still today. I'm still learning from gifted dancers in my classes and rehearsals about the multitude of ways in which one can be integrated, compelling, vibrant, and aesthetically whole, about the infinite variety of movement choices one might make.

In terms of choreographic structure and form, I think Sokolow was the big, big influence on me because she kept paring things down and paring them down. She wanted intensity and yet she didn't want anything that seemed superfluous or extraneous. And she insisted on total commitment to the moment. And so, by learning some of her works, by seeing others and by teaching and reteaching one of her pieces, *Lyric Suite*, I learned much about integrity and simplicity and form. When I formed my own company, Anna gave me the rights to restage and perform *Lyric Suite* as a gift, for as long as I needed it. By immersing myself in that remarkable work, I learned some things that I deeply value about form.

Um, who else?...again, I have to go back to Cole. He made dances for many Hollywood films—*Kismet, Gentlemen Prefer Blondes, There's No Business Like Show Business*...I just love watching those gems of craftsmanship. I'm not necessarily talking about their content— mostly it's their structure and the integrity of execution that earn my admiration. His dances were never too long. If something was there, it was there for a reason; it was developed. There was nothing extraneous. And in Cole's work, and also in Sokolow's, the performer always pulls the audience in to them. They never throw themselves out to you. And that became very important to me, too.

[*pause*]

Q: What are some of the major challenges you faced along your journey to this point and, along with that, what are some of the choices you had to make? What were some of the difficult ones? Are there choices that stand out as exceptionally good ones? Are there choices in retrospect that you might have made differently?

BE: Well, I've made lots of big, big, big errors of judgment and some rash decisions during my life. At this point, I have a pervading sense of serenity, but it evolved gradually over many years and is not something I experienced for the first four and a half decades of my life.

From the mid-seventies through the early eighties, the Bill Evans Dance Company experienced phenomenal success. I had assembled an incredible group of former students who became a dazzling and passionate performance ensemble. I mean, almost overnight we were among the most-booked companies in the country. To my amazement, I received a Guggenheim Fellowship, and several fellowships and other grants from the National Endowment for the Arts. My company received many grants from Utah, Washington, King County, and private funding agencies.

The most exciting thing was that young dancers from all over the country graduated from college and then moved to Seattle to study with me, and many of them have stayed there to build a vibrant modern dance community. In Seattle, they call me the "father of modern dance." Now, even the "grandfather."

Anyway, by the early eighties, I had worked very, very hard, and achieved *everything* I had ever wanted...*except the ability* to enjoy it. Deep inside, I felt unworthy of all the success I was experiencing. Eventually, an overwhelming sense of shame caused me—subconsciously—to undermine my own success in the world. And I suffered agonizing loss and pain.

Q: The self-esteem issue seems to be a battle for many dancers.

BE: Yes. Kids of my generation who were born gay grew up with a cellular conviction that we weren't good enough. For me, it was the body language of my parents, my brother, and other family members...and, it was the thousands of abusive slurs and insults hurled at me by my Lehi classmates. I became convinced that I was a "bad" person, that I should feel ashamed. No matter how hard I worked, no matter how much success I experienced, I just couldn't ever feel worthy.

Finally, in my mid-forties, my years of silent self-loathing caused a total meltdown. Unbelievably, I lost my Seattle company and then my school. My seventeen-year personal/professional relationship with Gregg Lizenbery, which had been my bulwark, crumbled. I came close to a complete nervous breakdown, even considered taking my own life.

I was so stunned by those losses that I finally had to begin facing the demons that had tormented me since childhood. I had to learn to understand that I am, and always was, a good person.

So, for me, the challenge has been internal, the challenge of finding ways to acknowledge and confirm my self-worth.

In fact, I've had extraordinary success for a person growing up in the time I grew up, in the place I grew up. But it wasn't until maybe in the last decade that I was able to fully recognize that and say, "Yes, I deserve it."

This isn't necessarily answering your question, but over the past twenty years, I've learned to become a catalyst for positive change among others in my various corners of the world. When I teach now, my primary goal, and the primary responsibility I feel for every student who comes into my world, is to try to help her recognize something good about herself and claim it. I don't usually tell her what those good things are. I usually try to facilitate a process through which my students come to discover themselves and learn to validate what they admire about themselves. To me, without self-esteem, other things aren't all that important.

A course I've been teaching here at the University of New Mexico for a number of years, called Introduction to Movement Analysis, is really a chance for each person to go inside and start to understand herself on the level of developmental movement patterns and know that each one of us is quite an amazing being and that each one of us is okay, that each of us deserves to be seen as and valued just as we are. I sometimes remain silent throughout much of this process, as the classmates validate each other's uniqueness, and then I see all kinds of things start to happen for people, once they start to understand that they're okay.

Q: They feel it.

BE: They *know* it on a cellular level. They start to know that they're good people and that they belong...that they're part of something positive and larger than themselves, and then they're able to move forward.

A lot of the reason why I was finally able to come to this point in my own life was the practice of the Bartenieff Fundamentals, as I evolved my own integration of various Bartenieff patterns with other somatic work. It's largely through this work that I've become whole and well.

Q: And that helps with your decision making?

BE: Absolutely! I feel that the practice of Bartenieff Fundamentals has completed the wiring in my brain. I was born six and a half weeks prematurely, in a car, feet first, and suffered multiple birth injuries and entered life with many developmental deficiencies.

I can't make self-destructive decisions anymore because my practice of developmental movement therapy has made me whole. I now realize that I have a right to make choices that are good for me. I haven't had a self-destructive urge in a very, very long time.

Q: Now you recognize that that's what they were?

BE: I do. But I don't even regret them now. I don't regret them because that's who I was, and I had become that person for real reasons, and it was a growing process I had to go through to reach what I have become—knowing who I am and feeling good about who I am. I now know what it means to be happy. I can even find joy and satisfaction now by remembering the accomplishments of my former self, when I was still tormented.

So, I try to be the kind of facilitator for students that was missing in my life. It's the reason I love teaching now. I think I can be a catalyst for students' positive changes. I'm not doing the work for them. I mostly create an environment where it becomes possible.

Q: That's wonderful. And what are some of the major ideas that you would want to relate to dancers struggling to survive in the dance world? What would you like to tell them?

BE: Well, these are questions that come up daily. I have students who are physically gifted and dynamically expressive. And yet they're constantly thinking, "Do I want to do this, or should I become an accountant?" Well, yes, if this question comes up for you, you should be an accountant. If it's not something that feeds you on a deep spiritual level then, of course, don't become a dancer. I mean, dance recreationally, but, if you are going to dedicate yourself to dance, you need to know that you *must* do it. It's not something you can make a decision about. You simply recognize, "This is who I am. I am an expressive artist. Moving my body to manifest my view of the world is all that will complete me."

Q: But don't you find that there are students who get sucked into all of this other stuff: the parents, the homophobic society? Or they want it, but they don't allow themselves to want it?

BE: Or they don't yet know themselves?

Q: Yes, but they're still showing up at your doorstep like little orphans.

Bill Evans (standing) and Tim Wengerd, in Repertory Dance Theatre production of The Intiate, *choreographed by John Butler, 1969*

BE: Well, yeah, yeah…sort of.

Q: So, how do they come to say, "Yes, I must do this"?

BE: Well, as you know, I knew I had to be a dancer when I was a very young person. I mean, as I grew up and was influenced by guidance counselors, I tried to convince myself to do other things that might have pleased my family more or have been less frightening or offered more financial security. But every time I checked in with my heart, things became clear again.

Q: Well, if a person allows him- or herself to go through this process of exploration, going back to who they are on a cellular level, perhaps this question wouldn't be so difficult.

BE: Definitely. Certainly, for some, recognizing the profound need to dance can be a gradual revelation. As teachers, we need to help our students learn how to listen to their hearts.

Q: So, once you know you want to do it, what else?

BE: Well, you have to be diligent and self-forgiving. What I started to do about a decade ago, in every circumstance, is ask myself, "Well, did you do the best you could?" If I did, I say, "Feel good about that." Now, I may have failed in the eyes of others. I might not have completely achieved whatever it was I was going for. But if I did the best I could, then I experience serenity and can let it go. And that's all that we can do. We have to keep putting ourselves out there, keep taking risks and keep forgiving ourselves if we don't get exactly what we were going for. And we have to stop thinking, "I'm no good," or, "It will never happen for me." But every day, we have to stay open to the possibility of positive change and be honestly in the moment, doing the best work of which we are capable under the circumstances.

Our culture does not validate dance as a serious performing art or dance as a spiritual activity. Most people in our culture are afraid of their bodies, afraid of what they might discover when they start to learn about themselves on a body level. And so, when we decide to become dancers, we're combating so many things that are deeply ingrained in our culture that it can't be easy. It's never easy for anyone…but the struggle can be joyful.

What else…? I guess find a soul mate, at least one soul mate. Find someone who understands what you are about and who values you and who *you are*, not just what *you do*. Someone who doesn't judge you but will be there for you and might give you a push from time to time.

And then, know that your search for artistic satisfaction and a way to make a living are probably going to be difficult. It's going to be a struggle. Finding the funds to support your work can be a tremendous struggle. You have to be resourceful. You have to keep your eyes open.

And you have to believe in yourself.

I didn't learn to believe in myself until quite late in my life's journey. I had a lot of quick and relatively easy early successes. And then when I had to really struggle, I thought life was really unfair. I should have been really happy for those early successes and I shouldn't have been surprised when I encountered difficulties, but I had not been taught how to recognize my worth and claim my power.

I think one needs to know dance history. You can learn about the struggles of other artists. Even knowing that they have struggled can help you feel not so alone. So having a view of the larger context helps.

Q: Do you see a significant trend in any aspect of the dance field, either in training or in the attitude of people in the field or in the people perceiving us? In the subject matter that people are dealing with in their choreography?

BE: Well, yes…young people inspire me and amaze me and give me hope for the future of humanity. The people in my classes are mostly courageous and vibrant, and I feel blessed by the universe to be able to serve them as a teacher.

Something that comes to mind frequently is that young dancers have available to them longer, healthier careers. People starting to dance now, people in their teens now, can have lengthy careers because of the pioneering exploration done by dance teachers, scientists, and movement analysts, including me and many of the people closest to me. I think that's a great cause for celebration for each individual and also for the field.

In the past, too many people stopped dancing too early. I mean, there have been a few people who were able to go on for long periods of time; there's Erick [Hawkins] and Daniel Nagrin, of course. But, unlike the other arts, where many people have gone on for long periods of time, we haven't seen that very often in our field. So, we have not had significant numbers of role models who are older, people who have the kind of serenity that I'm experiencing now, still out there dancing. I think we'll soon begin to see many artists who continue to grow and remain visible in their senior years. To me, that's a wonderful evolving trend.

I think more dancers will want to be more politically and socially aware. At least I hope that there will be more of a return to social consciousness among young choreographers. When I was in my thirties particularly, I made political statements about the world: about homophobia, about the military industrial complex, about the arrogance of the white patriarchy. I had to get these comments out and the only way I was given to do it was through my art. Now, I don't mean to say that this is what you have to do as a choreographer, but when I was first discovering my personal voice as a choreographer in my early thirties, those were the pieces I had to make.

I would like to see more young choreographers who are politically aware and socially concerned enough to make those kinds of comments. If art and dance remove themselves from the larger world, they lose their relevance. And there again, I come back to Sokolow. She was extremely politically aware. I was with her when Robert Kennedy was killed. She said, "It's up to the artists to save society." Those were her first words! She believed it. And whether or not it is possible, is not the point. But the fact that artists believe that their work is powerful enough to be relevant to the larger world and to change it, is important.

Q: Do you think that this has something to do with your generation?

BE: Yeah, I'm sure it does. If I look at the students in my classes today, many of them don't have a sense of being empowered or that their work could make a difference. My impression is that they often think that their work is mostly for themselves and for their close friends. I don't usually find them motivated to make statements for larger contexts.

Q: Do you have a dream for dance for the future? For yourself for the future?

BE: Well, the other night I had a conversation with one of my colleagues at UNM [University of New Mexico]. She had been invited to choreograph the Mozart *Requiem*. So the Mozart melodies

Photo by Keven Elliff

Bill Evans teaching Bartenieff Fundamentals® at his annual Dance Teachers' Intensive in Port Townsend, WA, 2002.

started going through my brain and I woke up in the middle of the night just remembering how deliriously happy I was when I was choreographing my version of the Mozart *Requiem* on my own company for the first Dance Magnifico, part of Albuquerque's annual Festival of the Arts. There's something so magical about having a group of dedicated dancers and having wonderful music and being this kind of vessel for something coming together and people moving harmoniously in relation to each other. Then I thought, "Oh, my God, if I can't continue to do that, what a loss for me." So, even though I've disbanded my professional company, somehow I've got to continue to find ways to make dances that aren't teaching vehicles, but are created for their own intrinsic artistic value. Somehow, as I continue in life, I've got to have opportunities to do that. And then the other thing, I want to write about what I've done, what I'm doing, what I believe. Because all of what I've done won't be complete, especially for me, unless I reflect on it and make meaning of it. I want to do that.

Q: And a wish for the dance world?

BE: The dance world? Okay. Well, it has to be that dance becomes available to every child in the culture. That's my wish. The reason that I came to live in New Mexico, besides my need to be close to this awesome natural beauty, is because I had visited some of the Indian pueblos. I had seen whole communities of people dancing together, with very young children and the oldest people in the community, all dancing together. And something inside me moved and I thought, "Oh, my God...I've been missing this my whole life." A whole community where people dance together to recognize life's most sacred events. Every child in our culture deserves the experience of dancing. That's my wish.

Q: If you had to pick reasons why you are still in this field, what would they be? What keeps you going? What's still driving you?

BE: Well, I have never once questioned the intrinsic value of dancing. I've questioned the validity of everything else in the world.

Right now, for example, I'm dismayed by the American diet, our consumerist society, and the kind of hegemonic culture we've become. But I've never questioned the validity of what I do as a dance teacher, performer, or choreographer. It just seems innately noble to me. I think that teachers are the noblest people on the planet. And I think *dance* teachers are way up there.

Q: Way up. Shamans!

BE: Yes, our material is life itself, because life is movement. And so, I have never questioned the validity of it. Not to say I didn't question *how* I did it, but the acts of teaching and choreographing and performing, I never questioned their importance. It makes me feel that I'm making some kind of positive difference in the world every time I get to teach a class or perform for someone. I mean, not a spectacular difference. But if one person is more alive, has more belief in herself or in the beauty of life itself by what I do, it's worth it.

Q: Thank you, Bill. Thank you very much.

NOTES

1. Bharata Natyam, a solo classical Indian dance form of religious origin, is believed by some scholars to be more than 3,000 years old. Performed by female temple dancers known as devadasis as a form of devotion, it was codified in the nineteenth century in the courts of southern Indian by four brothers known as the Tanjore Quartet whose musical compositions for dance form the bulk of the traditional Bharata Natyam repertory today. Today the style noted for its blend of rhythmic and mimetic elements, virtuosic footwork, and extensive vocabulary of hand gestures is performed by men or women in solo concerts, often lasting three hours, or it is blended with Western dance and theater productions.

2. Mabel Ellsworth Todd (1880–1956) developed an approach to movement training called ideokinesiology based on the concept that the body moves as a result of a mental image. Her student, Lulu Sweigard, taught for many years in the Dance Division of the Juilliard School in NYC, applying Todd's groundbreaking body-mind approach to professional dance training. Irene Dowd, a student of Sweigard's at Juilliard, is one of the leading proponents of this approach to dance training today.

3. Batsheva, founded in 1964 by Baroness Batsheva de Rothschild and Martha Graham, is the most well-known modern dance company in Israel.

4. Effort/Shape was an early name for the portion of the Laban-based movement theory dealing with movement dynamics. It is more commonly known in the United States today as part of Laban Movement Analysis or Laban/Bartenieff Movement Analysis.

5. Irmgard Bartenieff (1890–1981) was a student of the Hungarian movement theorist Rudolf Laban. In 1936, she fled Nazi Germany arriving in the United States, where she applied her Laban training to the field of physical therapy, eventually developing her own approach to body re-education called Bartenieff Fundamentals.

Courtesy of Madeleine Nichols

Madeleine Nichols

MADELEINE NICHOLS

"...So, how do you measure your work? You measure it by their success. That's it. That's all you have your eye on. That's fun!"

As curator of the Dance Collection at the New York Public Library for the Performing Arts at Lincoln Center from 1988 until her retirement in November 2005, Madeleine Nichols has been a vital force for the dissemination and preservation of dance information, history, and materials. Coinciding with her important work at the library, Nichols has been a dance research educator, having shared her knowledge as an adjunct professor for New York University's program in dance and dance education for over fifteen years. Nichols is also an attorney. Her legal work focuses on issues of copyright, contracts, and estates as they relate to the rights of performing artists. She has served as chair for both the arts section of the Association of Colleges and Research Libraries, a division of the American Library Association, and for the New York Public Library Research Libraries Council, and has been on the board of directors and editorial board of the Society of Dance History Scholars. In 1992, Nichols helped to found the Dance Heritage Coalition. In 2006, Dance/USA and the dance community honored Nichols's many years of commitment to the documentation and preservation of dance and her persistent efforts on behalf of dance artists' rights by awarding her an Ernie, which recognizes "unsung heroes" in the field of dance.

SETTING THE SCENE

Although it was unplanned, Madeleine was the perfect finale to my interview journey. We met in her office, tucked away in the back of the vast holdings of the Dance Research Collection of the New York Public Library. As always when I have had an opportunity to speak with Madeleine, her clearheaded thinking and eye to the future made me pause and reassess my own perspective on dance once again. Hers is a generous and macrocosmic worldview, one that encourages a person to dream and think *big*, allowing the dance world to be just that, big—big enough for everyone's dreams.

— R.C.

Q: Well, Madeleine. You are the last of my interviews. So, here we go! How do you describe what you do to other people? For example, if you met a group of kids or people who didn't know that much about dance?

MN: That happens all the time and I wish I could have twelve words or less to describe it. Everyone wants to know what a curator is. "What is that?" In a museum sense, a curator is understood, and that's part of my job. The other part of my job involves information service for a very specialized subject that has a comprehensive research library collection. We collect materials, all kind of materials, and then from that pool of materials, we display them with the help of the museum staff that's here in the building. Then I ask people questions about what I've described. Because some people understand it and some don't.

Q: What kind of questions do you ask them?

MN: It depends on the audience and upon whether or not it's a family member, or someone in the library world, or someone in the dance world. If it's someone in the library world or other research areas, historians, or people who do that kind of academic research, they are interested in the fact that we communicate all the time with people through the Internet. In addition to dealing with people in person, we use the Internet, and e-mail, and the telephone. Actually, more people use this library off-site than come on-site. And that's been the case for about ten years. *That* amazes people. The world is changing so fast and we get librarians that want to see it in action here. This is a very exciting place if you are in the library world or if you are a historian or in any of these traditional areas, because we are dealing with far more than books.

If you are coming from the dance area and you are either a choreographer or dancer or are producing shows, then you want to know how this applies to you. How can you use it? If you are a choreographer, say, in South America, here's how it works. You somehow come to this country, you find this place, and you see that we're really eager to have some photographs and programs,

MADELEINE NICHOLS

165

videotapes, or some kind of documentation of choreographic works and other dance activities. It doesn't have to be theatrical, proscenium concert dance. It can be any kind of dance. And the minute you get that information to us, we do what libraries do. We catalog it, it goes up on the Internet, and the choreographer or dancer in South America can say to family, friends, and other presenters there, "See, they recognize me, you should, too." If this lends credibility to an international event, well, that's an easy thing for us to do with our regular resources. We don't need anything extra; it's very simple. It's one thing this library has to add to the field.

The other thing it adds to the field is something that Jerome Robbins had a vision for, understood, and used this library for. He felt that dancers and choreographers needed a place where they could see other styles of dancing, pure styles of any kind of dancing. There's not a limit to what we think is dance. For us, it can include gymnastics or ice-skating. For example, there's a lot of religious and sacred dance catalogued here. Now you get very close to an anthropological perspective of dance and how it is viewed in culture. We then link to other libraries that are anthropology libraries. So we try to do that.

What we are *really* interested in here is the *dancing*. What shows the dancing? What describes the dancing? What explains the context of the dancing? And if it is being overlooked elsewhere, now we *really* start to care about it, because otherwise it's going to be lost and we really don't want that to happen. That facet is a characteristic of the New York Public Library in particular. This library is one of the top five research libraries in the world. Depending upon how you're counting, it always comes up near the top and it has no national limitation as a national library would. It has no tuition limitation as a university library would. So it really fills in a gap. It has, for over a hundred years now, kept its eye on mankind's knowledge and how you get it and save it, and make it accessible so that people all over can do what they want with it. Well, now you know why I can't find my twelve words or less.

Q: I know. It's really great. I love it! So, this takes me into the next question. Do you consider your involvement in dance to be your profession, your career, your work, your passion, your calling? All of the above?

MN: Probably all of the above. When I studied dance, a hundred years ago, it was ballet, tap, and acrobatics. It was clear that I was not built to be a dancer. And what I thought was the most beautiful dancing, and what I wanted to be was what I saw, which was ballet... the photographs of Maria Tallchief...the Ballets Russes when they came on a tour to the town where I grew up. That was the kind of dance I really wanted to do at the time. And, of course, I couldn't. It wasn't going to work. And while I studied for it and took a couple of summers to study in New York, by the time I was a teenager, it was clear that I had to make a decision. Mind you, I had no other images of what dance could be. I had never seen something like José Limón or Doris Humphrey. I might have made a different choice had I understood that there were other kinds of dancing. I just didn't know about them.

So I stopped cold turkey in high school and went to college. And decided that *that* was what I was supposed to do. But I still think today that my brains might really be in my feet, with my tap dancing. But back then, I didn't want to become a tap dancer, that wasn't it.

Q: Well, it's never too late!

MN & Q: [*laughter*]

[*pause*]

Q: How did you first get introduced to dance and what have been some of the landmark events in your dance life? Who were and are some of the major influences and inspirations in your life?

MN: When I stopped dance cold turkey and went to college, I did find an entire other universe. I don't think I could have done

167

both. If I still had been dancing, I think I would have been totally absorbed by it. So how to put words to whatever that is, I don't know. But I know that by stopping cold turkey, I then looked at the rest of the world and found other mentors, other achievers in other fields.

Q: Who were they?

MN: Usually just businesspeople, friends…you know, occasionally you'd come across a teacher who was special…there was an English professor back at the University of Michigan who taught Chaucer. If I had to characterize them, they were people with high integrity and intensity of focus and excitement about what they were doing. That is the common thread in the people that I've met who've inspired me. The library field was simply a way a woman could sustain employment. So that is why *that* was attractive to me. So I studied that right out of college. Not thinking that there was any dance in that. But then, when there was work at the New York Public Library, already loving New York and knowing that I wanted to try to work in libraries, I came here. I didn't know where that would lead me. Imagine my surprise when I found out that at the New York Public Library, there was a special place for dance. That was *really* amazing! From this particular library, it's possible to look at the entire dance field around the world and to see what's needed, and to understand some trends and then to try to help when you can. So, I came full circle back to dance and I'm really privileged to be here and to serve in any way I can. Does that answer your question?

Q: Well…when you first started your dance training, was that at a local studio?

MN: Yes. This is what parents did for children then. They exposed them to piano lessons if they could, and they exposed them to dance lessons. I'm sure my mother wanted me to walk gracefully. Little did she know that I really liked using the large muscles of my body. I still do.

Q: And what were some of the major challenges you faced along your journey? What were some of the choices you had to make? Were there difficult choices? Were there some exceptionally good ones? Are there choices you would have made differently?

[*pause*]

MN: Because this is a hard question to answer, I want to tell you that recently I think of the world in terms of what marketing people call Generation Y and Generation X. I'm a boomer. Anyone over forty years old is a boomer. But from about twenty-five to forty is Generation X and under twenty-five is this Generation Y coming along. Your book is probably reaching out to the Generation Yers. Here's what I have learned, having gotten to where the boomers are now…the obstacles never go away. And it doesn't matter what they are. The more you do, the more the obstacles come. One simply learns to deal with them. If you are going down a road and you know where you're going, you're not so aware of the potholes. If you're going down a road and you're looking at all the obstacles, the potholes, all of them, that's all you'll see. And you'll stay there working on all the potholes and you won't get down the road. So it's a trick, really, to keep your vision, whatever that is. And where does vision come from? That's a hard question to answer. I don't know.

I think the challenges people have, give them an exercise. So, maybe there are physical challenges, maybe there are personal challenges, in family structures and so on. In a way, they really don't matter. What matters is what you do confronted with those challenges and how you manage them. Whether you stay focused on what you are trying to do, whatever that is, or not. And that's almost a daily mental search, to go, "Okay, what is it? What am I supposed to do now? Why am I breathing? What am I good at? What do I enjoy doing?" That always gives you a clue about what you are supposed to be doing. Does it always work? No, it doesn't always work. I think that people do need a team of people around them, to help them go where they're supposed to go. They need some trusted advisers. That team changes as you grow. And you do grow. So, it's hard to answer these questions.

Q: Are there concrete examples from your life of obstacles that you faced?

MN: In an overall way, I wanted to dance. Wasn't meant to. Don't have the body for it. And now, I'm probably doing something more significant for more people than I'm even aware of. I'm aware of the people I'm dealing with transaction-by-transaction here in the library, but I know that what we are doing overall is impacting other people that I've never even seen. *That's* probably what I'm supposed to be doing, because dancing was different than I thought it would be. So, there's an obstacle that, you know, in spite of myself, I'm still in the dance field in ways that I never would have been able to understand or imagine.

Q: And obstacles as a dance curator?

MN: Obstacles as a dance curator? Hmm…I'm in a large, highly structured organization. This is good and this is bad. My personal style is that I like to work fast. I was brought up that way. That's what our family dinner conversation was like. A ping-pong game. No one ever finished a sentence. [*laughter*] Now I come to see in the rest of the world, that's rude. So that's been an obstacle and I still work with that.

Q: So, what are some of the major ideas you would want to relate to dancers who are struggling to survive and thrive in the dance world? What would you like to tell them?

MN: I would encourage them to never, ever give up on what they want to do. There's a cartoon that someone sent me about ten years ago. It was from an acquaintance in Philadelphia who saw that those of us in the library work long hours at a terrific pace. There's not very much pay and we are constantly busy. The cartoon is of this large bird. I think it's a stork. Its bill is tilted upward and it's trying to swallow a frog. The frog's back legs are hanging out of the stork's mouth and its front legs are around the stork's throat, firmly wringing its neck and preventing the stork from swallowing the frog.

170

As long as the frog holds on, the stork can never swallow it. And at the bottom it says, "Never, ever give up." That's what Winston Churchill said at commencement addresses, I think, during or after World War II. "Never, ever, ever give up." So it's true if you know what you want to do and you know it's the right thing to do. You have to really grab on to that.

The encouragement for me can come from lots of places. Here I am in a library. So encouragement can come from books, or you see other people who have done it. You see other stories. For example, here on my bookshelf is a story of a man named Dale Fern. He was a very bright student in a farming family in the midwestern United States. As a high school senior, he was offered a college scholarship. His family was very proud of him and very much wanted him to go to college. However, he had seen in his high school *library*, *Dance Magazine*. And in *Dance Magazine*, there was a picture of Olga Spessivtzeva. He had never seen anything so beautiful in his life. He wanted to meet this person. So, against his family's wishes, he came to New York City instead of going to college. He had heard that people in New York City would know where this creature was on earth. So he came to New York City and he started asking people, "Where is Olga Spessivtzeva?" Everyone was very evasive, but he never gave up.

He took dance class after dance class, as people do when they come to New York. At every studio he went to, he asked all the students, he asked the teachers, he asked the people who ran the schools about Olga Spessivtzeva. Finally, through his persistence, people began to understand that he was serious about finding her. He collected every photograph, every old article he could find of Olga Spessivtzeva. Well, he ultimately found out that she was in a mental hospital in upstate New York.

When he made the first visit, he had been told to take, I believe it was, oranges, chocolate, and stockings. Not stretch, but silk stockings. Which he did. When he got there, she was quite disheveled. It was a state institution and she was quite withdrawn. He didn't know what to do because he couldn't communicate with her. So the next visit, he brought a Russian priest, because he thought

Courtesy of Madeleine Nichols

Madeleine in a tap dance recital photo

the Russian connection would help. And, of course, it did, because no one had been able to understand her and no one understood her ballet background.

He kept up these visits regularly. I believe he went up every Sunday or every other Sunday on a train to see her and slowly but surely, she began to come out of her shell. The place where she was began to work with her more and understood then that the Russian language was important. Well, the Tolstoy House finally took her in. One of the things she did in her old age was to make these very beautiful dolls—these figures. One of them was Nijinsky in his famous *Giselle* costume. She gave that to Dale Fern and that's now here in the library, with the photographs that Dale Fern collected in loose-leaf notebooks. Are they rare vintage photographs? No. Are they put together by someone with passion? Yes! And they tell you more about Olga Spessivtzeva than all the books in the world would.

So, that's a story of a person who never gave up. He was never made to dance. He made his living in New York as an actor. He's not famous. You don't know his name, but the story...

Q: Wow! [*pause*] And if you had to pick a few reasons why you are still in this field, what would they be? What is it about your dance life that keeps you going?

MN: Oh, it's the people...it's the people. Dancers are particular. Artists, in general, are the most special people on earth. They've been given talent, insight, abilities, and a vision that the rest of us don't have. They see things in a way that the rest of us mere mortals don't. They help us see better, they help us understand the world we live in differently. Often, they have a difficult time because they're not comfortable with the rather *brutal* way that the rest of the world works. They find that offensive. They're probably correct. But it's the only way the rest of us seem to be able to manage at this point. So, I love working with the artists. That's very exciting. Every once in a while, they come needing something. And if you can feed that need, then they go on to create something. One of the special things about working in any library, not just this library, is that your work is intended to help other people succeed. So, how do you measure your work? You measure it by their success. That's it. That's all you have your eye on. That's fun!

Q: Do you see any significant trends in any aspect of the dance field, either in training, in attitudes of people both in and out of the field, or in subject matter that artists are dealing with?

MN: There are some trends. People are working on projects over a longer period of time than they used to. Teachers are working individually with students more closely than they used to. That's interesting.

Q: Taking a longer time with projects, similar to what Graham used to do?

MN: Possibly…but, similar or not, people are working on their projects over a period of years. Another trend that's obvious, is that we're moving into a digital world…

Q: We're in it.

MN: We're in it and we can't even see it. Even Generation Y can't see it. There are trends within Generation X and Generation Y that are truly enlightening for me. My hunch is that the reason dance is going to be sustained (for those that are interested in it) is that it has to do with more than just "B for ballet" or "T for tap," or whatever style your dance is. It has to do with relationships and communication, and in a digital world, that becomes the economy. That becomes the way it works. That becomes the *energy* of it. Dancers obviously, as a part of their art, understand retaining energy and expanding and letting the energy go. That is the physics of the universe and that is the electronic world we are living in.

Everyone reading your book is going to be living in a time where we're in two worlds. We're still in this chemical world of photographs and all the tangible things. But we're also making it into this digital world. This transition is tremendously exciting. Young people now, Generation X and Y, have relationships that are lasting over periods of time, in a close way, far more than the baby boomers. The Internet, e-mail, is helping them do that. They are keeping their friendships. Fewer career jobs exist in today's world. Dancers may already be accustomed to that situation. [*chuckle*] That doesn't mean that it's good for the dance field, but it is simply a fact of life now. The forty-year plan, where you went to work and you were there forever, is really on the way out. In fact, it is highly unusual. With the communication among young people using the Internet, the relationships are tremendously important. They are helping each other get jobs. They are helping each other find where they should go next. That's pretty exciting and wonderful. And I think that's going to be an asset to the dance field. Dancers are going to be way ahead of other people because this has been the terrain for dancers from the very beginning.

Q: And also the obvious, which is now we can document.

MN: Now we can document. And here, I have to sigh. You asked me about a challenge before. We are not documenting nearly as much as we should be. I still remain quite frustrated by that imbalance of quantity as well as quality. I thought ten or fifteen years ago that this library would not be needed in the documenting of performance. *Wow* was I wrong! Not only are we needed, sometimes we are the only one doing it! Presenters have not filled the need. The formal companies themselves have not filled the need regularly either. They're trying, but some of them don't have enough money to buy new tape stock. Or they are using equipment that's obsolete. Everyone is using equipment that's obsolete at this moment. But we're close to breaking through with some standards for that. So that's going to come along, but it's still a very big obstacle.

This past century, though, joyfully, is the first century where we were able to see the real thing. Photography gave us the ability to photograph the dancer and the body. So, the image has not gone through the painter's hand or an engraver's hand. We've got those from prior centuries. Those works convey powerful information to us, those pieces of art as it were. But with the chemicals and the photographs from this last century, that's given us a whole new lead on dance and what people see. Starting in the twentieth century, people saw photographs. Then people saw Fred Astaire dancing on film. Further into the century, even more people saw dancing on television. We don't see much dance on television now, but we do get to see dancing on MTV. That's not bad. We need more.

We need different styles of dancing available and I think that the economics need to be worked on just a little bit more. That is around the corner.

Q: When you say "obsolete," what do you consider not obsolete for those artists filming their works today. Is everyone switching to DVD and digital video cameras?

MN: The technical people who are providing us with information and equipment are saying the same thing over and over. "Do not put all your eggs in one basket. Do not transfer everything into digital right now. It's too early." Yes, banks have all of their information in electronic form. Yes, the music industry is now almost entirely in electronic form and is learning how to preserve that. But, there is not enough information yet for moving bodies and images in digital formats.

The New York Public Library is one of the founding members of the Dance Heritage Coalition. This is a very small entity. It is simply a group of people and institutions who see some of the problems of dance preservation and are dedicated to high-standard solutions. It's just a project-to-project venture and it's always within a hairsbreadth of going out of existence. But believe me, if you can get eight people from eight different kinds of institutions to agree that this is a serious problem, and to agree upon how we need to resolve it, then you have some progress. Slowly, we've been able to get some of these things at least identified. One of the most recent projects of the coalition is a test with analog videotape to see how it transfers to digital images and to see if that can be preserved and compressed in a way so as not to lose information. The difficulty of seeing a camera pan across a sunny grassy lawn, for example, is that all of the information that the analog picks up is not always caught in the digital. There is a scientific firm that has done some testing on recent footage from the Dance Division. It involves visuals of Gregory Hines tap dancing in white trousers. The fast movement of his trousers was hard for the digital format to capture from the tape. These are the kinds of tests that they've done and I do think they have found something now that exists in the marketplace that mathematically does not lose any of the information. That's what we're looking for and I think we've found it.

These are the kinds of exciting things that are happening. They don't always happen on our timeline. We want the answer to the question now and there is not a good answer today, August 2004. But if we can all get the word out and be expecting those requirements of our equipment and our systems, and keep an open architecture to our digital world, replacing these little analog boxes that are magical in themselves, we're going to be fine. We're going to be ahead of other fields.

It's the same way in the area of copyright. There was a gentleman here yesterday from the World Intellectual Property Organization.[1] He is working to raise consciousness about the importance of choreography and copyright. This is great for dance! I don't know where it will go. It will not go quickly. But it will proceed. It's a wonderful thing.

Q: It's an ongoing process then?

MN: I think it is inevitable to be quite honest with you. I actually think that we are part of an enormous tidal wave for dance. It will not be turned back.

Q: Well, that's great to hear! [*pause*] Do you have a wish or a dream for dance in the future, either personally or overall?

MN: I do. I wish dance were more accessible. That is, in the lives of every person on earth. If you live outside of the United States, most cultures do have dance as part of their everyday world. It's part of their culture. It's part of the way life is celebrated. But increasingly in the West, dance has become something separate, something only for the highly skilled, something only for certain bodies. That was my experience, for example. It is not in the vision of the day-to-day path. It is not in the sight line for most people. What is there on television today? There is MTV on television, but that's all. That's a limited scope of dance compared to, say, if you turn to Mexican culture.

For so many other cultures, dance is part of their heritage. Dance is the way the heritage is carried forward. In the United States, if we look at specific cultures that have immigrated into the United States (and they are everywhere), one of the ways that older generations have passed on their specific cultural heritage to their new family members is through dance. So, it's going on, but it's not in the mainstream. It's not in our shopping malls, it is not on the highways, it's not on our television, and it's not on the radio. Will we ever get to holograms? You know, where we just turn on our coffee table and there's a three-dimensional moving thing happening? That will be dance. That will be the art form. To have dance as part of the natural part of everyone's life. I would very much like to see that. So anything that goes in that general direction has my support.

Often, I watch with a great smile Generation Xers sitting for hours at their computers, many of them turning for recreation and social communication to swing dance. I mean, that's just one example. That's terrific!

Q: Any other thoughts, anything that you still want to say?

MN: Well, I wanted to turn around and ask you a question. Are there any similarities that you see with the other people you've been interviewing? Or are there any gaps and questions that you think are in the minds of Generation Y? You are one of the people who have been steadily listening and thinking about them.

Q: Well, there have been overwhelming similarities in the responses to a number of these questions. For example, when I've asked about all of your involvement in dance, everyone has responded that, yes, it is a passion. Everyone has mentioned that their mentors, all of them, had that similar intensity of focus. That's been across the board. It's obvious in the way you have all been talking about what you are doing. And when I ask, "Do you have anything to tell a younger generation?" everyone's been saying, "Don't give up. Don't give up. Don't give up!" And that's tremendously encouraging to hear.

And then, in terms of challenges (and I think this is the product of people who "succeed," in our sense of what success means), you have all been less focused on those. This group is not looking at or hasn't dwelled on, as you said earlier, "each pothole." They're part of the deal; they're not the deal themselves. And although everyone has been acknowledging money, or the lack of funds, you all say, "Yeah, money's a drag." But it seems as if everyone looks beyond that.

MN: It's not about money.

Q: It's not about money. Money is a factor, but it's not about money.

MN: If it's important to do, the money will come. That is a very frightening way for most people to think. And this may be part of an American framework, because we are economically aware. The free economy of the United States is one of the wonders of mankind. As frustrated as we might get from day to day with the economics and politics or any of the things that are in fact distressing, the fact that we're so conscious of the enterprise, may have us caught in valuing things according to dollars. Thinking that the dollars are what we need in order to do what we want to do.

I think artistically one must work constantly to follow that passion. To concentrate and to validate the passion. That's what the library can do for dancers. It can validate that very special interest they have. I have seen it time and time again. Two days from now, I will be welcoming about sixty incoming freshmen who are in a dance program at Manhattanville College. Well, what I remember from last year, having done this for the first time, is that virtually the entire incoming class was not from the metropolitan region. They were coming from all across the United States. In showing some materials, I was encouraged to see that all of the young men knew who Alvin Ailey was, and Nijinsky. That's not easy to come by in our culture. And then I saw the looks on their faces as they saw the kinds of books on the open shelves here, books that you can take out. When you see the encouragement they get from all of those dance books, all of those dance photographs, looking at a review of Doris Humphrey, for example, and imagining how she must have felt when she saw the review of her new work, all of these are validations of feelings they're having!

There's a biography of Isadora Duncan. It's called *Your Isadora*.[2] And very often dancers find in that book some similarities of thinking. The same thing happens with all the books on Vaslav Nijinsky. His diary, which was edited by his wife (her editing has come into criticism in recent years), and the later biographies and English translations of his diary, provide inspiration. When they see the struggle and the way in which he perceived the world, they completely sympathize with it. They find a kindred spirit there. Then they realize, "Oh, okay, I understand this." The rest of the world just often finds this really odd. But artistic people don't. It's important to validate those artistic feelings so that artists, dancers in particular, don't feel alone. Whenever that feeling, like "I'm all by myself," comes along, it's time to go find...

Q: Your tribe.

MN: Yes, your tribe, exactly. That's a wonderful way to describe it. It can be done very easily online.

Q: One of the things that's been frustrating for me in choosing only seven people for this book is that there are so many other people that haven't been heard from and so many other ways to be in the dance world that we haven't touched upon.

MN: Yes, you should keep a basket of ideas for this. Throw into a basket the names of people, whenever you think of them, the questions you wish you could ask this person or that person. Because I'm confident that there's a way that *that* interview can take place, whether you are the one doing it or not. It is important for dance to do this. Dance is a verbal art form. It's more than that, but it is passed from person to person. The words in dance are tremendously important. I happen to think that eventually people will be studying choreographers to see how choreographers communicate to get other human beings to enact the vision of the choreographer. Business schools have been studying the wrong people when they want to know about communication and team building. They need to study how choreographers do this. There's a huge variety.

We're in a time of such exciting flux; we have the capacity now to do things that we didn't have before. What if, for example, your readers were able to keep this going, by asking similar questions and new questions of other artists and people in the dance field of other generations? There are so many ways.

Q: Yes, well, dancers are accessible. Call them up. They'll talk. They'll most likely be flattered.

MN: They are accessible and not only are they flattered, they have information to give. You asked about future dreams earlier. One of the things I want to do is to increase the role of the dancer beyond that of an unpaid goodwill ambassador. Yesterday, a wonderful, highly respected, experienced, magnificent, contemporary dancer was mentioning that she felt that in touring many countries of the world, she was often an ambassador from one culture to another culture. Because while she is American, she was invited to other countries because they saw something in her work they wanted. She then in turn saw and learned from their work. I would like to see her *recognized* for her work as a goodwill ambassador. But I would like her paid for all that she does.

So, occasionally, when these interviews come up, and some wonderful gem of an artist who is healthy now and has credibility for what he or she does, well…that *ambassador* status could generate a book and residual rights for the artist.

And I want the dancers who are touring, I want them paid top dollar. I believe that there are ways to get this to work out. The copyright leaders of the world are wrestling with how you maintain economic action with copyright protection. This is a worldwide electronic situation; it's being worked out in the recording industry among others. But, as the gentleman from the World Intellectual Property Organization pointed out, those are all old models. Well, here's dance coming along and we didn't get caught in any of the old models. We were left out. Might this be our moment for new models?

So throw your thoughts in the basket and I'm quite confident that Generation X and Generation Y have ideas that will go way beyond what we're thinking. Pick a topic, almost any topic in dance, and it's pretty much wide open and full of lessons.

Q: And that's exciting. I mean, you can't say that about many other fields, that there are so many topics to chose from.

MN: Exactly. And what I really like about that is that dance is evolving on multiple levels, so that young dance students can pick a topic beyond the very well known and they can add to the observational knowledge. They can collect what exists. They can save what is going to be lost. And they can think ahead to what might be. We are developing academic thinkers. We are a little behind some other countries in our thinking process. But we are going to have some amazing thinkers who can assess and understand better the smaller topics, some things that are new, plus the broad overarching ones. And they're really going to be doing a great job. I see it changing. We're going to develop the philosophers of dance. We don't have them yet. There have certainly been a few along the way. But, by and large, until now we've had observational information that people have been trying to collect and assess. Going forward, this is changing…and that's really exciting!

Q: Madeleine, this is great…I think we can call it a wrap.

MN: We finally did it!

NOTES

1. The World Intellectual Property Organization, a specialized agency of the United Nations, was established in 1967 to promote the effective use and protection of intellectual property throughout the world.

2. *Your Isadora: The Love Story of Isadora Duncan and Gordon Craig*, edited with a connecting text by Francis Steegmuller. New York: Vintage Books, 1976, © 1974.

INDEX